Small House, Big Life, in 400 Square Feet

Tips and Strategies for Living in a Small Space

Megan Bryant

Table of Contents

Introduction	5
1 The Tiny House Lifestyle	7
Case Study: Andrew and Crystal Odom	8
Case Study: Brittany Yunker	33
2 Why Choose Voluntary Simplicity?	46
Case Study: Laura LaVoie and Matt Belitsos	66
3 The Tiny House Movement	84
Case Study: Deb Delman and Kol Peterson of Caravan—The Tiny House Hotel	99
4 How Consumer Culture Impacts the Movement	118
Case Study: Dan Louche and Kathy Truhn	119
Case Study: Christopher Carson Smith and Merete Mueller	143
5 The Path to Living Tiny	157
Case Study: Macy Miller	189
6 Designing a Tiny Life	208
Case Study: Lee Pera and Jay Austin of Boneyard Studios	222
7 Designing a Tiny House	247
Case Study: R D Gentzler	248
Case Study: Hank Butitta	277
8 Realize Your Dream to Live Tiny	292
Case Study: Andrea Tremols and Cedric Baele	305

INTRODUCTION

What is the function of a house? To many people, a house is where you sleep at night and keep your stuff. Naturally, people with this view will want to have the biggest house they can afford so they have room for a lot of stuff. This thinking may explain why in a time when family sizes are shrinking, the size of American homes is growing. Today, the average home is around 2,400 square feet compared to 1,500 square feet in an average home in the 1950s.

But what if you want more from your house than storage? What if you want your house to be a vehicle that helps you live the life of your dreams? It sounds lofty, but that's the goal of the tiny house movement. While many Americans seem to be bent on building the biggest houses they can buy, those participating in the tiny house movement seek to find the smallest living space that can accommodate them. This choice isn't because they live in dense population centers or because they don't have the money for larger homes; rather, it is the pursuit of a lifestyle that seems to be lacking in modern society.

The recent housing and financial collapse of 2008–2012 shook many of us and left people without jobs, without homes, and without retirement accounts. These harsh economic realities left many people questioning the status quo and seeking livable solutions they could afford. For many, tiny houses are a way to exit the traditional home mortgage, an escape from the rat race, or the means to a comfortable retirement that they previously thought was not possible.

A tiny house is housing with a purpose. We make the decision to live this lifestyle because we have taken a step back, considered the options, and realized it's the path for the life we wish to live. The tiny house movement is one in which average citizens are picking up hammers to build their own future. They are saying to the powers that be, "We aren't playing your game; we choose our own destiny." It is people recognizing that in their short timein this world, they want the freedom to live a life focused on what is important to them instead of a tying themselves to sixty-hour work weeks to maintain large houses full of stuff.

The tiny house lifestyle is one of financial independence, freedom, and ecological responsibility (these houses tread lightly on the earth). For these reasons and many more, people are leaving their McMansions behind and taking up residence in tiny houses to live life tiny.

Living in tiny spaces certainly isn't anything new to humanity; small dwellings are quite the norm for many people who live in cities or areas where real estate costs are high, or those living in situations that necessitate living small. What is interesting is the movement of people who are consciously choosing to live not just small, but tiny. This movement marks a major shift in thinking and living for people across the globe. Despite pressure from the society we live in, people in the tiny house movement are turning to these alternatives and living the life many of us dream of. It is a life that we choose, not one that we are forced into, which is empowering.

Many people will find it ludicrous to live in a tiny house, but those who live in tiny houses find it crazy to live in anything else. While we are a bit fanatical about tiny houses, we realize that living life so small is an extreme. It isn't for everyone, but we hope to at least spark a conversation about the life we live and question how we live it. This book is full of ideas that will help you understand, embrace, and apply the principles of the tiny house movement. Whether you downsize to a 400-square-foot home or simply scale back the amount of stuff you have in your current home, you'll learn how to live well with less, which is a freeing idea.

THE TINY HOUSE LIFESTYLE

People have tried to define exactly what a tiny house is, and these definitions have brought much debate. But trying to define a tiny house is missing the point. Tiny houses have sparked the imagination because they have taken housing to a place that many people had never even considered. To some, the mere fact that there was an alternative to large homes didn't even enter into the realm of possibility. The movement has built houses that many thought were not possible. It has brought back a design sense that has been lacking in most housing built in the past thirty years. It has carefully evaluated what humans need from the environments in which they live—which are often not taken into consideration in today's traditionally built homes.

Case Study: Andrew and Crystal Odom

How It All Started

Andrew and Crystal Odom's life in a tiny house started out with a simple question—"what if?"

"What if we didn't see wants as wants, but as goals?" The Odoms asked themselves this question at the beginning of their marriage, when they were saddled with debt and looking forward to the life that they wanted to build. They reasoned that transforming a "want" into a goal would motivate them and help them create an action plan to achieve what they wanted.

Their plan was practical and an interesting departure from the culture of conspicuous consumption that Andrew was participating in before his marriage to Crystal. Andrew describes growing up in a culture in which you went to school—college if you were lucky—with the goal of getting the highest paying job possible so you could "consume in a conspicuous fashion. You consume to show others how successful you are," Andrew said.

It's a culture that shows its prosperity through material goods. Before his marriage, Andrew had done his best to consume conspicuously, spending his paychecks and taking on debt for an expensive new truck—purchased with the intent to impress and fit in. Andrew said he felt social pressures to be the provider for his family, and that culturally he believed it was his duty to provide a big house, expensive vehicles, and the best clothes so other people could see how he had "made it."

As a result, Andrew brought a large amount of debt to the marriage. Luckily, Andrew figured out that he wasn't obligated to participate in the culture of consumption that surrounded him. The Odoms realized that they were the best judges of their own personal success and that they could decide for themselves what would make them successful instead of following their culture's definition of success.

One of their ideas of personal success was to be debt-free, so they aggressively paid down their debt and then started to build the life they wanted to lead.

Making the Decision

Andrew had realized it was time for him to walk away from the culture of conspicuous consumption, but the newlyweds still needed a home of their own. They had been approved for a home loan of almost $200,000, something that would have been a mark of success for Andrew in the past, but Crystal helped him stay on track by reminding him that their personal definition of success was to be debt-free. With that goal in mind, they explored all sorts of alternative dwellings.

They had wanted to build a small cabin, but realized with the zoning laws and other factors, it was going to cost a lot of money for such a simple house. For the acre plot of land that they owned in eastern North Carolina, they saw a lot of opportunity. They considered yurts, park models, and finally tiny houses. Building a tiny house on a trailer was a way for them to avoid much of the costs that came with dealing with codes, zoning, and related requirements.

When they started thinking about the features and characteristics they needed in their home, they went through a process of examining their lifestyle. A lot of their time was spent outdoors, and they mostly just needed their home to be a place to sleep and to prepare and eat meals. They both had lives outside the home.

Crystal had just finished with mission work and her possessions were limited to a backpack. Andrew had sold much of his belongings to pay off debt, so the two of them had very little to start their new life. This made the transition into tiny house living easy because "you don't need a lot of space to put things if you don't have a lot of stuff to put somewhere," Andrew said.

Currently, Andrew works from home. He often works at quiet places in his community (during this interview he was at a workspace at his local library). He plans to build a separate small home office soon because he spends most of his time away from his office.

They were able to pay for their home with cash and built what they could from what they had on hand. Freedom from a mortgage has allowed them to save for their next projects: building Andrew's home office and saving for a tiny house for their daughter.

Accommodating a Child

The Odoms were just about ready to start building their tiny house when they found out they were going to have a baby. While having children has deterred many people from building a tiny house, the Odoms decided to continue with their plans and simply adjust the design to include an area for the child.

Raising a child in a tiny house isn't as difficult as people imagine, the Odoms say. Their daughter is still young (two years old at the time of the interview) and the house can easily accommodate all three family members. They have a designated space for their daughter's things. In the future, as their daughter grows up, they plan to build a separate tiny house for her so she can have her own room but still be close by.

They are selective about how many toys their daughter has. If there is a toy their daughter is not playing with, it finds its way out of the house. "We try to keep things minimal not for the sake of being minimal, but for the sake of why does this kid need all this stuff because the more stuff she has, the less imagination she uses," Andrew said.

Allotting Storage Space

When it comes to storage, the Odoms' tiny house meets their needs as a family in a variety of ways. In general, the family just doesn't have a lot of space. Each member has an allotted amount of space for his or her.. personal things. Crystal and Andrew each have a small nook where they keep a wooden box of important keepsakes and things that have significant sentimental value. Their daughter has a space with some shelves for her books and toys.

Their main storage area is a 4'×4 closet that serves as the clothes closet for the entire family. This closet holds only the current season's clothes. They swap out their winter and summer clothes seasonally. Off-season clothes are stored out of the way in a small shed.

They also have what they call a "garage," a small storage space built over the tongue of the trailer and accessible from the outside of the house. This space is where they store shoes and extra items not used on a regular basis.

While the Odoms don't have a lot of material possessions, the items they do have are very high quality, which means they will last longer and work better, and they will need less in the long run. When it does come time for something new, they make sure that they use the "one in, one out" rule to help keep things in order and make room for everything.

Daily Life in a Tiny House

The Odoms describe daily life in a tiny house as more intense. "When it's romantic, it's more romantic; when it's angry, it's more angry; when it's comical, it's more comical. Everything is amped up," Andrew said.

Living in a smaller space has made them more aware of each other's personal needs and caused them to be more courteous when one of them needs space. Andrew views his family as an intentional decision. His wife and daughter are the people he wants to be with, so he enjoys spending time with them in the small space. While there are times when there is stress in the home, Andrew believes these stressful times occur less often than if his family lived in a typical-sized house.

Andrew said living in a tiny house has made him more aware of the importance of cultivating relationships. He now devotes the majority of his time and energy to his relationships, and as a result he has seen a big difference in them. He realized that before he moved into a tiny house he used to buy affection in his relationships through gifts and other tangible goods. It's a trend he believes is common in American culture. "We all are guilty of it at some point," he said. "We buy a gift because it's the easy way out."

While the family still exchanges gifts, it's only a few gifts to which they have given a lot of time and consideration. When they buy a gift for their daughter, they make sure it's something that will enlighten her, something they know she will use regularly, and often they give her an experience she would enjoy rather than a physical object.

They also have more leisure time together as a family. Instead of spending their weekends doing domestic chores, the way many of Andrew's peers do, the Odoms' housekeeping takes mere minutes. It takes about seven minutes to clean all the flooring in the entire house. The small kitchen cleans up quickly, and there is less stuff to put away because there isn't much stuff to begin with.

The biggest change a tiny house has brought to the Odom family is financial independence. "If I lost my job tomorrow I'd be sad but I wouldn't be devastated," Andrew said. "Life would keep on going. Each month my family would have a roof over our heads, guaranteed."

With their financial goals met, the Odoms are now able to focus on other goals. They are planning to travel more as a family. Crystal and Andrew are going to finally go on their honeymoon, and they want to be able to offer experience and opportunity to their daughter.

Zoning and Legal Issues

Many areas have building codes and zoning regulations that make tiny houses illegal. The Odoms worked with local officials in their hometown in eastern North Carolina to come to terms that gave their tiny home legal status as a residence.

Andrew wants to see more tiny houses come into the fold on legal issues. He would like to see tiny houses become accepted as legal homes. He agrees with the growing sense that there needs to be more self-regulation among tiny house owners. He would like to see responsible tiny house owners build homes in more urban and suburban communities and become contributing members of those communities rather than tuck their tiny homes off the grid in the countryside.

Tips From Andrew and Crystal

- Changing your definition of success will allow you to succeed. It's not necessary to chase consumer culture to be successful.
- High-quality goods will last a long time. If you only have a limited amount of space, it's best to be choosy.
- Realize that experiences and memories sometimes make better gifts than objects.

What a Tiny House Is—and Isn't

Today's homes are designed for maximum square footage so people can fill them with stuff. We build three-car garages for our vehicles, huge walk-in closets for all our clothes, and formal dining rooms that are dined in only twice a year. Today's traditional houses serve not only as places to store stuff but also, in a weird way, as places that pay homage to stuff. Traditional design focuses on where to put stuff within the home rather than identifying how people interact with the elements of the home—how the home makes us feel and how designs can compel us to connect both with each other inside the home and with the outside world.

What makes tiny houses stand out over most of today's houses is their intentional design and their use of space, materials, light, and function. Tiny houses are both beautiful and functional. And while they provide a comfortable lifestyle, they avoid the trappings of consumerism. It takes a lot of self-reflection to be able to live in a tiny home.

The journey toward living in a tiny house prompts many questions. What is important in life? What are my needs and wants? Where do my wants come from and how does consumerism play into this? It is these questions and many more that make a tiny house more than just a house;

it's a place that requires you to foster a lifestyle that you both choose and seek.

So, while there are many competing definitions of a tiny house, understand that tiny houses have made a name for themselves by taking existing definitions and turning them on their heads.

I would generally define a tiny house as a home that meets the following three principles:

1. It focuses on effective use of space.
2. It relies on good design to meet the needs of the residents.
3. It serves as a vehicle to a lifestyle that the resident wishes to pursue.

Many are keen on placing a specific number of square feet to define a tiny house, but I think size really depends on many factors and we shouldn't pigeonhole ourselves to a number. Building a tiny house on a trailer has been a popular style and until recently, the size of the trailer determined the size of the house. Because of Department of Transportation regulations, many people seek a trailer that can be towed down most roads without special permits. This means that a house built on the trailer can be no wider than 8.5 feet, no taller than 13.5 feet, and the length can vary depending on the state in which the trailer is registered. So those who want to trailer their tiny house are limited to less than 340 square feet for their home.

However, some people are willing to seek special permits for their tiny houses on trailers. The 340-square-foot limitation was quickly turned on its head when people started receiving permits for wide loads. There are now tiny houses that are built using several trailer modules, combining two or three individual tiny houses to make up a single house. Other tiny house residents have worked with their local code enforcement to build their tiny houses on traditional foundations. Some even use the tiny house as the core of the home, while utilizing traditional outbuildings for additional living space.

I think the most important thing to understand when it comes to the question of how many square feet are in a tiny home is the size of the space relative to the number of people living in it. This means a single person living in 200 square feet and families of five living in 1,200 square feet are both living in tiny houses. Both homes require the residents to be intentional about the space they live in, including how they design and arrange it and how they use the house as a vehicle, to live the life they wish to live. Herein lies a key point that many don't understand about tiny houses: A tiny house is not just a home—it is a lifestyle.

In general tiny houses are so small, they're extreme. Most people don't expect a tiny-house advocate to acknowledge that tiny homes are quite radical in their approach. So why do people who live in them go to such an extreme? It is because today's housing status quo doesn't meet our goals in life. We find that in order to "keep up with the Joneses" we must give up too much of what we hold dear in this life. People who live in tiny houses have assessed the current situation of housing, time, money, relationships, and well being and determined that in order to achieve what they want most in life, they must radically change how they approach things.

What Has "Living Large" Done for You?

Some may think living in a tiny house requires too much sacrifice. Maybe that's because we've been told that having the biggest, the best, and the most of everything guarantees happiness. Let's look into this "guarantee." Census numbers show that an average American household will bring home an annual income of around $51,000 and between 33 and 50 percent ("Shelter Shock: Who Can Live by the 30% Rule?" http://www.mint.com/blog/housing/shelter-shock-who-can-live-by-the-30-rule-0113) of that income will pay for housing. This is a sharp increase from the 1950s when only 26 percent of annual household income was spent on housing. Remember that the size of the average American house is increasing (now 2,400 square feet) while the size of the average American family is decreasing ("American Households are Getting Smaller—and Headed by Older Adults" http://www.marketingcharts.com/wp/topics/demographics/american-households-are-getting-smaller-and-headed-by-older-adults-24981). So the average American is chasing a bigger house but carrying a bigger housing bill in the pursuit.

Today, the average American has more stuff than ever before. As a society we have been purchasing things at an ever-increasing rate. And while we've increased our rate of consumption, we've also increased the rate at which we dispose of things. In the average home, people either stop using or throw away an item within six months of purchasing it. Yet we could spend years paying off the credit card debt used to finance the items. It is a vicious cycle.

So why do we buy so much? To a certain extent it isn't our fault. Marketing psychology has progressed to a point that compels us to buy, buy, buy. Politicians have been urging the public to get out and stimulate the economy with shopping. Holidays are becoming ever more commercialized where we take gift giving to a whole new level.

There is, however, more to this overconsumption than just fancy ads, politicking, and holidays. Recent studies have identified the shopping experience as a stimulant that gives the buyer a "shopper's high." This shopper's high isn't figurative but actually quite literal. The act of buying something you want stimulates pleasure centers in your brain, releasing endorphins and creating a strong reinforcement pattern. This pattern is something that advertisers and merchandisers have long known about and taken advantage of because they can turn a profit. Further reinforcing this behavior is the use of credit cards.

Credit cards have been shown to allow people to cognitively distance themselves from the reality that they are spending actual money. In a time when making a purchase required a person to barter or trade goods, or even exchange physical currency, the person's "shopper's high" was mitigated by the reality of giving up tangible goods for whatever it was the person wanted to buy. In other words, a person experienced an immediate loss in connection with the immediate gain of the new item, making it easier to measure an item's true cost and worth. Credit cards remove this immediate sense of loss, making the "shopper's high" that much higher. However, when the credit card statement arrives at the end of the month, that sense of loss can feel that much greater, especially if one has overspent.

So what are the results of the pursuit of the most and the biggest? Almost half of Americans regularly spend more every month than they earn. Reports show that the average American household owes over $15,000 to credit card companies ("American Household Credit Card Debt Statistics: 2013" from Nerdwallet.com). This is in addition to car loans, student loans, and home lines of credit. So the net financial result is debt—but what's the net emotional result? Does having all this stuff and a big house to keep it in make us happier? Studies indicate it does not.

All the stuff you accumulate actually has a negative effect on your happiness. While consumers get that initial high, the resulting stress of paying for the purchases later and the clutter they create in their homes weighs heavily on them. Recent studies conducted by the UCLA Center on Everyday Lives of Families have shown that people are overwhelmed by clutter to the point that the clutter severely prevents them from living the life they wish to lead. This study found that only 25 percent of surveyed individuals could park their vehicles in their garages; the rest couldn't because their garages were too cluttered to allow room for parking. Think of how common it is to drive through a suburban neighborhood and see the cars parked in the driveways while the garages are filled with stuff that often won't be used for years, if ever, before being tossed away.

But for many people, the clutter doesn't stop in the garage. One in eleven Americans use self-storage facilities to contain their extra possessions. This booming storage business has taken off in the past decade even though the size of houses has grown at the same time. So not only do we have more space to store stuff in our homes, we are buying so much that we rent out more space to keep it all. According to the Self Storage Association, there are 2.3 billion square feet of storage in self-storage facilities in the United States in what is a $22 billion industry.

It is obvious that we have a lot of stuff. What's not so obvious is that this stuff is costing us a lot and ultimately leaving us unhappy. As all of these statistics show, bigger is not necessarily better. Once you understand the debt and stress the typical American life entails, you can begin to understand why tiny house residents have decided to take a different path. Living tiny does require some initial sacrifice. You're giving up lots of space and stuff you don't use. But you're also giving up debt, clutter, and overconsumption. Doesn't that sound like freedom?

The Potomac Cabin by Charles Finn, located in Missoula, Montana. Reclaimed metal is used to create a new house with a weathered look.

The entryway, with stairs to the loft.

The living room of the Potomac Cabin.

The reclaimed wood interior.

Living for What Is Important

The baby boomer generation is reaching retirement age, and many in this generation are giving serious contemplation to how their lives have played out. While working hard, earning a living, and contributing to society are still important, many people are realizing that being too career-focused comes at a cost. It means you're not able to spend time with the people you love or do the things that inspire you. In the end, many will look back and wish they had spent more time with friends and family instead of slaving away in a gray-wall cubicle. Unfortunately, the pursuit of more things often leaves people with no choice but to slave away at their jobs. Everyone realizes that debt requires money, but few people realize that debt consumes time. It can take years of hard work to pay back everything one owes, and while you can always make more money after you're out of debt, you can never make more time.

Many people reaching retirement age are trying to make the best of the time they have left. And the good news is that younger generations are learning lessons from those who came before them by examining the previous generation's choices and the outcomes of those choices; they are, in essence, looking at the cause and effect. The younger generation sees that the previous generation purchased large homes and as a result took on too much debt, which resulted in the collapse of the housing market. Many younger people see this as a cautionary tale and are giving up the pursuit of a big house in order to avoid the same fate.

People are recognizing the high costs of consuming more, not just in terms of money, but in strained relationships, happiness levels, stress levels, increased health issues, and sleepless nights filled with worry. Something about tiny house living clicks when people begin to wake up to these realities, when they begin to realize how short life can be, but more importantly how precious a gift it is. People decide to dramatically change their life's trajectory and purpose. They expand their worldviews to places they've never considered before. They decide to find their true purpose, whatever it is. And they understand that in order to achieve the life they wish to live, something big needs to change.

The realization that life is for living, not having, can be triggered by many things—being laid off from work, losing everything one owns, having a bout with cancer, or losing a loved one. Some people experience these things firsthand and others witness someone else going through it, but the result is the same—a desire for change. This change may not come right away, but the trigger event sets a series of events in motion that lead you to a life worth living. What is amazing about that journey—no matter how, when, or for how long it is—is that it is always exactly what you need right then and there. The lesson you learn can sometimes be tough; it might be that you never want to be in that same spot again, but in the end, the lesson is valuable and you survive. So, throughout this process of learning lessons, seeing the path, and taking steps to change our lives, how do we end up in tiny houses?

Tiny Houses as a Vehicle to What's Important

The end of your journey is not a tiny house; it's living the life you truly want to live. A tiny house is simply a vehicle that can get you on that journey to the life you hope to achieve. The reasons a tiny house is such an effective vehicle are because in addition to being beautiful, well designed, and modest in space, it allows you to achieve your dream while still addressing the necessities and realities of everyday life.

The reality is living any kind of life requires time and money. There will always be bills to pay, taxes due, and obligations to fill. The issue is how much time and money you want to devote to maintaining a lifestyle. When you think creatively about this, the question you ask shouldn't be "How can I get more money to have the great life and the big house?" but rather "What can I change about the way I play the game in order to achieve the things I want?" When you think about it in this context you begin to see where there are assumptions made about life that might not be correct. You realize that the things you considered to be mandatory parts of life were simply suggestions or direct copies of how someone else lived. You no longer take it for granted that the way things are done are the correct way (or only way) of doing things.

There is a simple story that illustrates this: A daughter was helping her mother cook a roast. As the mother showed her daughter how to prepare the roast for the oven, she took a knife and cut off one of the ends. The daughter asked her mother why she cut the end off and the mother responded, "That's how my mother always did it. That's how I have always done it." Some time later, the mother is visiting with her own mother and says, "Your granddaughter asked me why I cut the end off a roast before I put it in the oven. I said I did it because that's how I saw you do it. Why do you cut the end off?" The grandmother laughed and replied, "You cut off the end of your roast? I cut it off because the pan I had was too small to fit it." The moral of the story is it's important to fully understand a tradition, custom, or the status quo before you carry it on and apply it to your life. It may be something that benefits you, but it may be something you can do without or do differently.

As you look at ways to change the way you play the game of life, look for the things you can change that will have the most dramatic effect. Very often when people are unhappy with things in their life, they try to make changes but on too small of a scale. While it is progress, cutting the occasional dinner out isn't a life-shifting change that moves you forward. Look for ways to change your spending, identify the largest expenses, and then question how you could eliminate them. If you cannot make a lot more money, spend a lot less. For some, rent or mortgage takes a third to a half of their incomes, so if they can reclaim that portion of their income they can make strides toward living the life they wish to live.

Obviously tiny houses let you quickly reclaim the portion of your income devoted to housing while still serving your need for shelter. So you are meeting your needs, but suddenly not having to pay for it in the form of rent or mortgage. In a way you can see it as almost like getting a 30 to 50 percent raise because you no longer need to be a slave to that monthly payment to the bank or landlord. And while peoples' income tends to increase over their careers, rarely does someone make that large of jump in income. What is more, if you eliminate your housing payment early in your career, you can take the money you are saving and compound it over time, leading to huge returns beyond anything you would normally be able to achieve.

In addition to saving you money, a tiny house also drastically minimizes your risks. A mortgage has a certain amount of risk associated with it because, if at some point you fall behind in payments, you can lose your home and all the equity you've put into it in a foreclosure. Because a tiny house costs less, you can own one outright very quickly, removing the risks of foreclosure or eviction. What's more, tiny houses are seen as nontraditional housing and therefore aren't viewed as assets by banks and courts, meaning they aren't likely to place liens on your tiny house or repossess your home.

So we begin to see how this one shift in living will lead to a vastly different trajectory in life. This new course is made possible by tiny houses, but what is important to remember is that it's not enough to simply move into a tiny house. To achieve the life you want, you will need to make lifestyle changes, examine your beliefs, desires, and goals, and reconsider your spending habits. A tiny house is only a vehicle. Your choices and actions control where you go.

Case Study: Brittany Yunker

How It All Started

A few years ago Brittany found herself having time to reflect on the life she wanted to lead when she came home from her seasonal job as a guide in Patagonia. "I didn't have a job lined up or a place to live when I got home," she said, "but I had some money saved up all in cash that would be hidden in my shoes, backpack, and clothes as I journeyed back to the United States." This got her thinking a lot about what she wanted the rest of her life to be like. So she began researching options on the Internet and found tiny homes. She knew that if she got back and life got started again she would lose that momentum, so "while in Chile I bought the plans from a website and then the fireplace I wanted and had them sent to my parents' place," she said. "A thousand dollars later I knew I would be forced to be committed."

Living in small spaces wasn't anything new, since Brittany had worked on boats and grew up in an 800-square-foot cabin. She knew that she could handle the small spaces and how to live in them. When it came to building her house, it was an entirely new experience, though. She had taken woodshop class in the eighth grade and made a coat rack, but beyond that she had no building experience whatsoever.

Challenges and Opportunities

The toughest part about building a tiny house wasn't the physical aspect or working long hours, Brittany said. "There is the mental aspect of building the house where it looks like a house and you're excited, then you go inside and realize how far you have to go to finish the trim work." For her, the hardest part about building her tiny house was that at the time, even in the tiny house world, there weren't a lot of them built. It meant that she had to learn a lot on her own because there wasn't anyone to ask.

It also meant that she had to explain and in some cases defend her choice for a tiny house because no one had ever heard of them. So she started building her house even when those around her didn't quite understand. "I'm more of the person that if I have an idea I'm just going to do it," Brittany said. "I'm going to go for it. I'm going to answer the questions later. I'll figure it out. Things will fall into place and it always does." The funny thing was that when she started there were a lot of questions that she didn't have answers to, but those around her were the ones asking, not her. She had faith that this was the right option for her and the life she wanted to live.

When she was building her house there were a lot of people who did question her. Brittany even began to worry that if she did finish it and she didn't like it, or if she didn't live in it long term, all the skeptics might have been right. But, after all the worry and hard work, she had a home that she loved—and that put all the skeptics to rest. "People would come into my house and say this is way more space than they ever thought!"

For Brittany, living a life without a lot of material possessions wasn't new to her. Having done seasonal work in some amazing locales such as Chile and Alaska, she had learned to live with little. It was when she came back to the United States that she felt pressure to join in the consumer culture and it wasn't quite right for her. She said that after coming back from one of her trips, "I remember going shopping with some of my girlfriends after I began living in my house. They were going gaga over all this stuff and it made me think of what I needed in life." The upshot of this situation was that she was able to use her tiny house as an excuse to not participate in all the consuming, but still got to spend time with her friends.

For Brittany, it was "almost freeing to have this scapegoat of the tiny house." She does still enjoy shopping with her friends, but it's in a very different way. Each thing she buys, she has to consider what it will take the place of. With only a limited amount of space in her small closet, she has to choose what she will give up if she wants to buy something new. This leads her to be very intentional about her consumption, and it also means that she loves everything in her wardrobe.

Even with her home being quite well suited to her, Brittany noticed that it led her to engage her community more because she would use communal spaces around town to do more things in. Instead of having large groups over, she would meet them at a local bar. She goes to local coffee shops that have wi-fi.

Making the Plans

When it came to determining what she needed in her house she considered the things she did the most. Things that she used or had a need or function for the most often made the cut. With these things in mind, she could "justify putting in that small of a footprint." She knew that she wanted a place to cook her dinners, a place to sleep, a place to bathe, and so on. She knew that she had a lot of things for her hobbies. She skis, bikes, camps, and hikes—each activity had its own equipment that takes up space, so she designed her storage with that in mind.

During the day her table converts into a desk. She designed a little nook to store her laptop when she didn't want to think about work anymore. Upfront is the nook where she can relax, read a book, or just spend time in the space. The biggest modification that she made to her plans was her main closet space.

She designed a larger closet that had two doors. She knew from living in other smaller spaces that if she could see lots of little things, it makes the space feel smaller. With the doors concealing the contents of the closet, it allows for a cleaner look. It makes her feel like the house is cleaner, simpler, and doesn't stress her out as much as if it were open shelving. This allowed her to have all the things she needed in the space, but keep them out of sight and out of mind.

Brittany thinks that the plans she made fit her life at the time, so the layout of things worked really well for her. One major change she made was to create a sense of open spaces. So she opted to not have a wall separating the kitchen and the living room. She often entertains in her tiny house and has cooked and served dinner for six people at one time.

How Tiny Living Impacted Brittany's Life

Brittany felt that living in her home gave her freedom. Because she worked seasonally in other locations, or might want to take trips abroad, she could up and leave for a month or two without worrying about paying rent, she said, but she still had a place to come back to when she was home. "That, especially as a young person, was really freeing."

She also found that she had to work less, but could still enjoy life as she had done when she was earning more money. But it went beyond just maintaining the status quo. She was able to actually have more opportunities while she wasn't working. Whether it was spending more time on things she loved or traveling more, the tiny house enabled her to do more with less. Even doing all of this she was able to save more than she ever had, which meant that she could enjoy her time with less worry about bills and saving for retirement. "It was a lot easier to focus on relaxing, to focus on myself, to focus on what I wanted to do with my life," she said.

Brittany felt that her relationships were strengthened because of her decision to live in a tiny house. For one thing, she couldn't do it all in that space. A really big dinner party, for instance, meant she helped plan it with other friends who had a larger space. But even building the tiny home required her to become humble and ask for help to do things she didn't know how to do.

But having a tiny house and having to work less meant Brittany had more time available so she could help her friends more if they needed a hand with a project, if they were moving, or if she just needed to be there for a friend in a time of need. She could focus on what her friends needed and could provide it in a way that she could have never done if she had been working more.

Turning a Home Into a Business

One of the other reasons that she has been able to work less is that she now rents out her tiny house as a hotel. She lives with her boyfriend while her house is being used as a hotel. The extra income from her tiny house has had a major impact on her financial situation. Since opening up for business, she has recouped the cost of the house and then some.

Even though she never intended for the house to be a business, it evolved in a way that she could have never imagined. While she was away working in Alaska, a friend had asked if she could rent the house and it worked out well. So she started thinking about renting the house out and having it become a tiny hotel. The concept took off and she now has a great small business. With this new venture, people now are able to spend a few nights in her house to see if tiny houses are right for them or can just enjoy a unique hotel experience.

Since opening up shop, at least ten different guests who stayed in her house then took the plunge and started building their own tiny houses. "It is really fun reading the guestbook after people stay in the tiny house and see all the excitement they have about the house," Brittany said.

Her youngest guest was a seven-year-old boy with his father. The young boy was a "tiny house nut" and loved tiny houses. He would spend his time drawing his own tiny houses and looking at them online. The child found Brittany's website and the father secretly booked a weekend in the tiny house for him and his son. "The dad didn't tell his son where they were going on their weekend trip," Brittany said, "and when they showed up at the tiny house the son freaked out!"

It's stories like these that Brittany has come to know in her daily life. They show her how a simple little house can have such a big impact on her life, from earning a living to connecting with friends and family to inspiring the next generation of tiny-home builders. A decision to live a simple life has led her on a path that she never could have imagined.

Tips From Brittany

- Enclose storage spaces to make your space seem roomier. Instead of having open shelving filled with lots of little things, Brittany added doors to her closet to keep the clutter hidden.
- Consider unique solutions for additional revenue. Brittany rents out her tiny house to those just looking for a taste of tiny living, and it provides her additional income.
- Take advantage of the additional time you gain from living in a tiny house to help others or pursue your own passions.

WHY CHOOSE VOLUNTARY SIMPLICITY?

One of the most popular questions I receive on my blog, The Tiny Life (thetinylife.com), is "Why would you want to live in a tiny house?" Reporters always ask me what draws people to a life that seems so radical in today's world. It is a good question, because it gets at the heart of the topic—that a tiny house isn't just a house; it's an intention with purpose and thought behind it.

There are many reasons why people are living tiny. In fact, each person who lives tiny probably has his or her own specific and unique reasons, but over years of talking with thousands of tiny house residents, I have seen patterns emerge. I love listening to these reasons because they tell the story of each person. I'll include some of these specific stories in this book, but first let's cover some of the most common reasons that people choose tiny houses.

Dan Louche

Photo courtesy of Dan Louche, tinyhomebuilders.com.

New tiny house built by Dan Louche in Atlanta, Georgia.

Photos courtesy of Dan Louche, tinyhomebuilders.com.

Dormers add space to the sleeping loft.

The kitchenette in Dan's tiny house.

A desk area creates space for working.

Photo courtesy of Dan Louche, tinyhomebuilders.com.

Time

Time is perhaps a person's most precious resource. Our time on this earth is short; it can go in the blink of an eye and we're never guaranteed more of it. While I have known this fact my entire life, as I get older, I more clearly understand the gravity of this reality.

I often ask people this question: If you had more time in this world and could spend it however you choose, what would you do? Give some serious thought to that question. How would you answer it? Write your answer in this book.

For many people, this is a simple question. But others have no clue how to answer it—they don't know what they would do with their time. Many people respond that they would spend time with loved ones. Others would choose to pursue a passion in life. Still others would use the time to learn something new or try something that scares them. Whatever it is, in a traditional lifestyle you normally would put your "extra time" activity off until retirement, but in the tiny house lifestyle, you can pursue it today. It's empowering to have the ability to pursue the things you want right now without having to sacrifice other things.

How does living in a tiny house give you more time? Because a tiny house greatly reduces your annual living expenses—the amount of time you must spend earning an income is greatly reduced. A tiny house lets you spend less time at work because you don't need the extra income. The lower cost also helps you get more enjoyment out of the time you do spend at work because you are free to take a job you truly love, regardless of the pay. If you find yourself in a job or place that isn't right for you, you can leave because you don't have to worry about making a mortgage or rent payment at the end of the month. You can hold out for your perfect job because you've been able to save all of the income that would have gone to pay for housing. This freedom puts you more in tune with what truly makes you happy and what you need to help you achieve that contentment at work. Tiny living strips away the clutter in your life so you can make better assessments of places to work and people to work with.

Working at a job you love pays off in so many ways. Your work improves because you're passionate about it. You can focus more on relationships with your coworkers and get more done because you love what you are doing. This level of passion and performance makes you extremely valuable to the organization where you work. You are very productive; you are a positive force for them. You lift up the other employees with your energy. So your supervisor and coworkers are willing to advocate for you and are more likely to support you if you choose to ask for a nontraditional schedule, work reduced hours, work from home, or even work remotely, which opens up the world for your exploration. Imagine being able to move to Costa Rica for six months while you live and work from a sandy beach. You still need to get your work done, but now your backyard is an exotic land to explore. Employers are willing to fight for great employees, and this gives you the latitude to ask for a work schedule that works for you, that allows you more freedom, that gives you more time with the people and things you love.

This increased free time and greater satisfaction at work (made possible by living in a tiny house) has a ripple effect that improves the overall quality of your life. Working less and enjoying work more greatly reduces your stress level. The work (and your free time) energizes you instead of draining you. It opens doors of new possibilities instead of making you feel as if you are facing years of drudgery.

Living in a tiny house gives you the extra time to do what you love and helps you enjoy your obligations more because you're able to meet them on your own terms (working at a job you love). A tiny house lifestyle gives you the flexibility to live as you see fit and walk away from things that are no longer for you. It opens doors that you never thought possible, all because you chose to live in a house with purpose.

If you had more time in this world and could spend it however you choose, what would you do?

Freedom

True freedom is the ability to choose your own fate and determine how you spend your life. It's a powerful force that resonates with the soul; it brings an internal harmony that few things in this world can match. Freedom is an inspiring force that breeds optimism, positivity, and faith in oneself, and these attributes breed success and a sense that you can create your own luck and fortune.

How much freedom do you feel you have in your life at this very moment? Could you walk away from your job tomorrow if it wasn't meeting your mental and emotional needs? Could you pack up and move across the country if you wanted to?

Without freedom, life is something to be endured and survived. Many people view life as just another workweek to get through, more bills to pay, and so on. When I talk to people who have the freedom to choose their own life course, I notice they all have one thing in common—they love life. With freedom, life is for living. It's an adventure. It's exciting. And it's always engaging. And they have that freedom because at some point in their lives they jumped up, seized an opportunity, and never looked back.

A tiny house is an opportunity for freedom that you can seize for yourself. In the western world you have the freedom to choose where you live. The first step to tiny house living is exercising your freedom from convention. Just because your neighbors are building bigger homes and buying more stuff doesn't mean you have to do the same. When you choose tiny house living you say, "Forget convention, my life is worth more." You are seizing the opportunity to live life as you see fit while choosing a path that lets you deal with the realities of life—bills, taxes, etc.—on your own terms. When you are free to do as you wish, your life has so much rich meaning to it. It is a force that makes you jump out of bed and say, "Hold on!" because today is going to be an adventure.

A tiny house leaves you free to pursue things that you always wanted to try. Many of the tiny house people featured in this book found the freedom to leave a corporate job and pursue their passions. Some might use their freedom to take up a hobby that has been a dream deferred. Others will use the freedom to pursue a business venture they've always wanted to try but were afraid to.

It is inspiring when people are able to take up the things that they have always wanted to do. There is a peace about them. What they create is often inspiring because they pour every ounce of passion they have into what they make, and when they talk about it their eyes light up. It is this experience that tiny houses can bring to you when you choose the freedom of living as you see fit.

So what is the one thing you have always wanted to do? What is the one experience you have always wished to try? What is that hobby you wanted to pursue? What is the trip you always wanted to take with your loved ones? Think about the life you could lead and think about how you can get there. *Tiny House Living* might be the driving force that allows you to get there.

Finances

For better or for worse, money makes the world go round, and personal finances are a reality that everyone must contend with. Tiny houses offer a huge cost savings compared to traditional homes and apartments, and this savings is one of the main attractions for many people. Some don't like the idea of a mortgage, others don't want to spend a ton of money on a large home, and others don't have a lot of money to spend on housing.

YOUNGER PEOPLE

The first group that is often interested in tiny houses tends to be in their late 20s and early 30s. Younger people have seen their parents and their friends' parents slave away at cubicle jobs only to be laid off; they have seen their homes foreclosed on; and they have watched them struggle to make ends meet even though they worked hard and were well educated.

It is with these life experiences that they seek tiny houses as a way to escape the rat race and the pitfalls of a large mortgage. This generation is markedly known for its focus on relationships and wanting to derive meaning from life and the work they pursue. It is no wonder that they are drawn to tiny living: This lifestyle helps them achieve all these things in one fell swoop and they are able to lead the lives they wish to live while still meeting the realities of adult life.

BABY BOOMERS

A generational group also defines the second group of people; it is the "baby boomers" that are facing retirement. These people have just endured thirty-plus years of work only to have their retirement accounts take a brutal beating in the stock market. In general, most of them hadn't been saving enough to retire, but with the market crash in 2008, what little they had was decimated. This, coupled with rising health care costs, leaves them wondering how they can retire.

The light of the end of the tunnel for these people—retirement—has gone dark. They are left trying to grapple with how they are ever going to be able to make it. They may turn to the idea of tiny living to bring the light at the end of the tunnel back into view. With this new approach, the game changes completely, and the numbers shift in their favor.

This group does have to make special considerations for the future, which might include accommodating wheelchairs and such, but a new class of tiny houses is being built to meet these needs. What a lot of retirees like about tiny homes is that they can live their lives as they see fit, but when it comes time to have extra care, they can park their tiny house in the backyard of their children's homes. It means that they can be closer to their family and enjoy spending time with their grandchildren. This way they can live in their own home, have their own space and privacy, but still be nearby loved ones who can be there when they need help.

SEEKING A BETTER LIFE

The final group of people that comes to tiny houses is those who simply don't have the funds to live in a traditional home. This can manifest in many different ways, but it ranges from people looking to escape homelessness to those who have been lifelong renters but want to become homeowners.

There is a great potential with tiny houses to help tackle the issue of homelessness. There is a strong potential for social justice when it comes to housing. Tiny houses on trailers have the added benefit of being mobile, so you can move your home to where you can get work, further helping people escape the grips of poverty and homelessness.

Some people, for a variety of reasons, are not able to generate enough income for a traditional house. It could be because of lack of job opportunities or it could be because they were injured on the job and have limited employment opportunities. For some, it is because of the shrinking middle class in America or because of generational poverty or because they had a devastating medical issue and subsequent bills. There are many reasons why people simply aren't able to afford a traditional house. A tiny house is something they could reasonably work toward.

With this group, the smaller strain on income a tiny house provides can empower them to make life-changing progress. It could be that the money they save allows them to pursue higher education; it may be enough to purchase a good suit for interviews at a job so they can increase their income; it could be that they save the money so they can weather bumps in the road of life; or it could be a life change that allows them to simply be able to put food on the table. Whatever the goal is, and however they decide to use the extra income, it can be an empowering force for their future.

Environmental Concerns

Many people also decide to pursue a tiny lifestyle because of environmental concerns. Many are beginning to see the toll humans have taken on the earth and they want to be good stewards to the resources it provides.

Traditional home construction usually encompasses a large array of destructive practices. Often, the first step of new development is to clear-cut the entire subdivision so it is bare ground. This practice destroys trees, vegetation, and wildlife habitats, and has many other unseen impacts. Lumber is often imported from other countries or far distances and the amount used is incredible.

What might be the most staggering fact is that the average amount of waste created by building a single traditional house in the United States weighs more than almost two tiny houses! Each traditional home creates in excess of four to five tons of waste that is entered into landfills.

Once a home is built, tiny houses consume fewer resources to heat, cool, and power themselves than the "greenest" or most energy-efficient traditional home could ever dream of. Since most tiny houses have such low power requirements, adapting them to green energy options is far more feasible technically and monetarily than traditional homes. There are several tiny houses that can power themselves on a single solar panel and a basic system that costs no more than a few hundred dollars.

It is when you make drastic changes in the lifestyle you lead in terms of material and energy consumption that you can begin to see how you could shape a sustainable future for generations to come.

Tiny house dwellers take this even further in some cases, moving beyond just reduction of resource consumption, but some are even able to achieve what many refer to as net neutral (no impact on the environment) or even net positive (goes beyond no impact, to improving the environment) houses. This means that through their building process and living, they utilize practices and processes that actually produce more energy than they consume, and they capture materials from waste streams instead of sourcing new materials.

There are many tiny house people who use reclaimed materials to capture valuable resources from waste streams, reducing their impact on the environment and saving money. The use of reclaimed materials has many pros and cons, but
for those who are seeking to lessen the impact that their dwelling has on the environment, it is a very good option.

One thing worth pointing out is that not only do tiny houses take fewer resources to create, but because of this, you can be more discerning with your product selection. When you are only using two hundred 2×4s to build your house, you can spend the extra money for responsibly sourced materials such as sustainably farmed lumber or alternative materials like SIPs (structural insulated panels) that would be prohibitively expensive on the scale of a traditional house, but in a tiny house, might only be the difference of a few hundred dollars. It is this latitude in the selection of materials that allows us to build responsible houses with higher-grade materials.

DIY Mentality

Many people who build tiny houses decide to build the house themselves for a variety of reasons. They are attracted to the idea because of cost savings, or like the idea of building things with their own hands.

This is a really interesting facet of tiny living, because common citizens are picking up hammers across the nation to build a new future for themselves. It is an inspiring image, people taking hold of their destiny in a sweeping movement of positive action. These people aren't skilled trades people, they don't have prior experience, and they may have never swung a hammer, but they are building entire homes!

We see many people who have never built anything in their lives but have a desire to build their own tiny homes. They are single mothers, white-collar workers, teenagers, and students. People you would never expect to are raising walls and creating a place to call home. Another thing that is interesting about this movement is that while the construction industry is dominated by men, women are building almost

60 percent of tiny houses.

While it is inspiring that so many people are taking on the lofty goal of building a house, there is also a need for training for these individuals. Building a home takes specialized skills and knowledge, all of which aren't in the normal skill set of most people who reside in white-collar office jobs. Up until now, many of these pioneers were tapping into their social networks and relying upon family and friends with this knowledge.

In recent years, we have seen a surge of training workshops and events designed to equip people with the skills, knowledge, and experience they will need to build their own homes. Along with a push for education, we are beginning to see the emergence of self-imposed building standards that are designed to keep people safe, yet are still approachable by the do-it-yourselfer.

In many cases, DIY houses are actually built better than most professional builders would do because the owners/builders are emotionally and financially invested in the project. When you are the builder and everything is riding on the house and you have to live in it, you pay attention to details and go the extra mile that some builders might not.

There are many quality builders who do amazing work, but not all builders hold themselves to the same standards. We have seen it time and time again in the building industry where a company takes short cuts, chooses low-quality materials, or rushes through a build—all in the pursuit of profit. By being the builder yourself, your goal is not profit: it is quality and safety.

Monika Petersen's Horsefly Cabin

Photo courtesy of Monika Petersen, mpetersenphotography.smugmug.com.

Monika Petersen's Horsefly Cabin in the winter in British Columbia, Canada.

Photos courtesy of Monika Petersen, mpetersenphotography.smugmug.com.

Rustic kitchen of the Horsefly Cabin. The kitchen island and small table are made of reclaimed barrels.

Custom timber dining area.

Going Back to the Land

There is a sizeable subset of tiny house people who are what many would characterize as "back-to-the-land" type of people and others who refer to themselves as "preppers," those who are preparing for potential disasters in the near future. While these groups are distinct in their definitions, there tends to be overlap in their motivations, so I include them together.

Many members of these groups are drawn to fiscally conservative and simpler ways of life. Tiny houses provide for both of these things because of their low cost and minimalistic lifestyle.

Back-to-the-land folks like a simple life because it lets them focus on being self-sufficient. Tiny houses are easily adaptable to being off the grid, they can allow you to live in a place without having to interface with local or federal government, and they can serve as a place to live while establishing a larger homestead.

Preppers similarly like the ability to be off the grid because they plan for a future where infrastructure will not be available because of an event that disrupts society. Since tiny houses are easily built and for not much money, they are seen as possible "bug out" shelters that preppers can afford to have without sacrificing their main homestead. Additionally, the flexibility of a tiny house in design and portability means that tiny houses can be location independent. So when an event like a natural disaster, economic collapse, loss of job, or something similar occurs, you can pick up and move to greener pastures, should the need arise.

Unique Spaces

The final reason people decide to build tiny houses is that they can create unique and beautiful spaces to live in that are nontraditional in many ways. You can put your own personal stamp on the floor plan, the design features, and the accents. Building your own tiny house allows you to have much more control over the design and creative process of your home.

There are many aspects of tiny houses (and the philosophy behind tiny living) that attract various types of people to this lifestyle, but we all seem to share a passion for simple living and low-cost housing. Perhaps the unique quality that attracts us is the cozy space that tiny living creates; it could be the simple lifestyle a tiny house enables; it could be the novelty factor of its size; the cost savings; the feeling of self-sufficiency one gets from building and living in a tiny house. Some have said—often in jest, but perhaps with an ounce of truth—that tiny houses actually fulfill a childhood dream of having an awesome fort or tree house. Having a small hideaway to escape to brings us back to a time when things were simpler. In the end, we are all looking to create a better life for ourselves, even if we have different motivating factors.

Case Study: Laura LaVoie and Matt Belitsos

Photo courtesy of Laura LaVoie and Matt Belitsos of Life in 120 Square Feet.

How It All Started

Waking up one day, it hit Laura that she couldn't keep doing her job for much longer. "It wasn't fulfilling me, it wasn't what I wanted to do, and no one was ever going to knock on my door and say, 'Hey, Laura, do you want to be a writer today?'" she said. She knew that she had to take steps toward her dream of being a freelance writer because no one else was going to do

it for her. It was the ability to move into her tiny house with her partner, Matt, that really gave her the courage to take that step.

For Matt, it was his search for how he wanted to live his life. After graduating from college, Matt quickly landed a job at a large IT company, where he was running a whole department. When he was twenty-one, he had achieved more than he ever expected to accomplish in his whole life, but this didn't fill the part of his life that he thought it would fill.

So, having achieved what he had set out to achieve—being congratulated by his peers and family—Matt remembers telling one of his coworkers that he wanted "to live in a house that I built with my own two hands on land that is important to me," he said. So he and Laura, though coming at this from different places, decided to take this journey to build their house together.

What they didn't know at the time was what exactly they would end up building. They knew what they had to change in life to achieve these things, but how they would get there was still a mystery. As a couple they explored cord wood masonry buildings, earth ships—all types of alternative housing options. Then a friend told them about a segment on tiny houses she had seen on *The Oprah Winfrey Show*.

Later Matt and Laura researched tiny houses and instantly knew that they needed to build one for their home. "It was small and it seemed like a buildable size for two people who didn't have a lot of experience building, so it kind of snapped into place at that point," Laura said.

Photos courtesy of Laura LaVoie and Matt Belitsos of Life in 120 Square Feet.

Approach to Building

They purchased plans for their tiny house since they had never built anything before. At the time they were living in Atlanta, but the land where their house was to be built was in Asheville, North Carolina. This meant a four-hour drive between where they lived and where they were building. So they traveled back and forth, working their jobs while they built a new life for themselves. It wasn't ideal, but they knew that they wanted to live in Asheville, so they made the distance work.

Building the house took them the better part of three years of weekends, inviting friends to come up and join in swinging a hammer. Some of the time they spent in Asheville, mixing work with fun. They frequented downtown Asheville, the farmers market, and various attractions of the area. So the long process of building was also spent enjoying the area while they pieced together their new life.

On serious workdays they relied on a work plan that they developed to keep things organized. They had a lot to coordinate living in Atlanta because if they ever forgot something at home, they weren't able to go back and get it. So each week they would sit down and say, "Here are our goals for the weekend; these are the materials we will need and the tools to accomplish them."

Their plan also helped them to have the right materials. The area where they were building their home didn't have a hardware store close by, so even trips to the store had to be planned carefully. Once they got their materials, there was the matter of getting them to the building site. Their house was being built partially up a small mountain, so it meant they had to hike a lot of the materials to the building site.

For Matt and Laura, building the house was an adventure that they could have together. They saved for a few years to purchase their land and pay for the house. For about thirty thousand dollars they got fifteen acres of land, a debt-free home of their own, and "three years of something that really gave us focus in our lives and taught us a lot about ourselves," Matt said. So for them it was an amazing deal: land, house and life direction. Many Americans hope to achieve these in their lifetimes but they achieved it all in three years.

Photos courtesy of Laura LaVoie and Matt Belitsos of Life in 120 Square Feet.

Living Off the Grid

In the end their tiny house was quite basic. The solar panel system powers a few lights, their cell phones, and their laptops, which they use to work from home. They carry in water from a nearby spring. It suits their life quite well because they have everything they need in that home.

Living in their tiny home they realized that what most of the United States sees as needs is really just a matter of wanting something. They had spent time abroad where they had seen how most of the world gets by on almost nothing. Beyond food, water, shelter, and the convenience of
the Internet to earn a living from home, they didn't
want much more.

There are things that Laura and Matt do have that many people in this world don't. "It makes me very appreciative of the things that we enjoy and I don't take those things for granted," Matt said. Even the opportunity to build a house for themselves was something they feel lucky to have done. Being able to achieve such a lofty goal in their lifetime is something that many people never do because life gets in the way.

Laura and Matt's Approach to Design

When it came to the design of the home, they took a lot of cues from the plans they bought but added their own changes to suit their needs. They spent a lot of time talking through the process of living in their (at the time) imaginary home. Even though they talked about it a lot and tried to think through living in the tiny house, some things did come up along the way.

A few times they realized that some things weren't going to work the way they had intended, so they stopped and dealt with it.

Photos courtesy of Laura LaVoie and Matt Belitsos of Life in 120 Square Feet.

Designing a Tiny Life

Since they wanted to work from home, they had to have a place to work. While they cooked a lot, they often opted to use their outdoor kitchen space. They needed a loft to sleep and a place to use the bathroom. Beyond that, they engage their community and spend time out and about in the place they love.

Since moving into their house, both Matt and Laura have changed a lot in their lives. Laura has since left her job and began her career as a full-time freelance writer. Matt still works for the company that he did before, but he sat down with his boss and explained how he wanted to make some changes in his life. Matt wasn't sure how his boss would take the news. "I told them what I wanted to do and if they were okay with it, great. If they said we think it's time to part ways, then that would have been okay, too," Matt said. In the end they agreed to keep him while he worked from the tiny house. That meant he could still earn the same amount of money, but now he did it in his own way from home.

With this new life, now that they were debt-free and could work from anywhere, a lot of possibilities opened up for them. "The whole point of getting rid of our great big suburban house was to reduce our expenses, and it made it possible to do what we wanted to do," Laura said. Things like their off-the-grid solar power system means no utility bills, and Laura was worried about how much health insurance would cost, but it turned out to be lower than she expected. So these things "enable me to work on my business," she said, "and even though I earn less than I did at my day job, I live quite comfortably."

They both count themselves lucky because their income hasn't changed too much but their living expenses have been reduced down to almost nothing. "It's something that I am grateful for every day," said Matt. They have much less stress now when compared to their old lives. While there are still some things in life that cause stress that you can't get away from, much of the unnecessary stress has been eliminated. Laura used to have a lot of stress from her old job; near the end the stress became very taxing on her. Now she enjoys her work, her life, and the lack of stress that comes with it.

"Reducing repeatable stress in the things that I like to do and then not having to do things I don't like to do was really important," Matt said. He has carefully designed his career so he does only the things he is good at and enjoys doing, because he feels that it's not worth having too much stress.

While they both earn a living, the time spent doing so is much reduced and the times that they do have work obligations they feel that it is more just a part of life, not a separation of work and life.

"The other day we were doing some work on the house," Matt said, "but we stopped for lunch and the guy at the counter saw that we weren't dressed for work and we were working-age people. So he asks, 'What are you two doing this afternoon?' It was clear to us that the unspoken thing was, 'Why are two working-age people not working, how could you possibly do that?' I have definitely seen that from a lot of people, because it's so hard for them to understand how it is possible. I understand that you have obligations to earn a living, but the idea that for every day, between the ages of twenty and sixty-five, you are going to go to this one place and do this one thing—that seems beyond bizarre to me."

Photo courtesy of Laura LaVoie and Matt Belitsos of Life in 120 Square Feet.

How Life Has Changed

The tiny house was "a vehicle to have a location-independent life," Laura said. "With the tiny house we have a place we can return to, but we also have the ability to explore all the other opportunities." They love Asheville, but they also plan to travel more and live in other places on an open-ended basis. The tiny house has enabled them to do this.

Matt and Laura recently spent time living in their hometown. Matt told me, "My mom is getting older and the holidays are a big deal for us. So spending time with those you care about without having to worry about what our employer is going to think or worry about rent was a big deal for us."

In focusing on relationships, they found a shift in how fulfilling their lives have become. Matt told me about how working on the tiny house with Laura had brought them much closer than they already were. It was building that life for themselves as a couple, literally and figuratively, that had a deep impact on them being able to live in such a small space as a couple.

Interestingly enough, they have grown apart from some relationships. Moving to Asheville means that they have had less time with their friends in Atlanta. Not having traditional nine-to-five jobs means that they can't relate to that life anymore, which changes the dynamic they have with some other people. So it can be hard to connect at times even with those who live around who do have traditional jobs, because while Matt and Laura have more time, their friends often don't. Their friends are only available after work and then are tired from working long hours at jobs they don't really like.

Growth of the Tiny House Movement

Since they first started building their tiny house, Matt and Laura have seen a lot of growth in the awareness of tiny houses. "There were no blogs when we started," Laura said. "Now there are tons of other people building tiny houses." She thinks that while people know about tiny houses as "cute little houses," most of them don't understand that there is a movement behind it—a movement that is seated in sustainability, financial independence from debt, and gaining a life where you can pursue your passions.

They feel that people are drawn to tiny houses for the benefits of that lifestyle, not because it is trendy. This organic growth has created its own movement.

Matt attributes part of that growth to the fact that now there are lots of examples available that have shown you can live a great life in a well-built home and not have to worry about housing prices, mortgages, or economic woes. "Tiny houses serve as a counterbalance to 'bigger is better,'" he said.

Laura points out that the movement has allowed people "to change their mindset, to realize you don't have to live in a really tiny house. So, ultimately, it doesn't matter so much the size of the house that you live in, but it does matter the quality of your life you have. And I think the tiny house movement is in many ways a poster child for that."

Photo courtesy of Laura LaVoie and Matt Belitsos of Life in 120 Square Feet.

Tips From Laura and Matt

- A tiny house is a vehicle to the life you want to live, not just a home. Make sure to prioritize what is important to you.

- Living off the grid is more expensive up front, but definitely cheaper in the long run.
- Tiny houses bring a lot of opportunities, so be ready to say yes!

Photo courtesy of Deb Delman and Kol Peterson of Caravan—The Tiny House Hotel.

THE TINY HOUSE MOVEMENT

The tiny house movement is still very much a grassroots-type of movement. It has grown quickly, but it is still really in its infancy and is sometimes still considered a fringe movement. It certainly has been gaining notoriety, mainly because of the novelty factor, the fact that the houses are well designed, and it's a lifestyle that appeals to many.

What is interesting is that tiny houses may have had the biggest impact on people who aren't necessarily interested for personal or environmental reasons. Since the economic crash in 2008, many people have been attracted to the movement because they are tired of the rat race or they have been burned by the stock market or the big banks, and they want nothing more to do with them.

A Growing Movement

While we who are in the movement don't want or expect everyone to live in tiny houses, we think that it has a valuable function in our society by showing that there are other options to be had. For many who find tiny houses, it opens their eyes to the fact that there is a lot to be improved upon in the housing market.

People are also beginning to see that they might consider a smaller space to live in. While it may not be 100–200 square feet, some are now considering 800 square feet over their palatial 5,000-square-foot home for two.

Another key thing that the tiny house movement has been able to highlight for the general public is the value of good design. When we look at most of today's newer homes, we see structures that often don't have well-thought-out design. People are looking to have well-built homes that create a sense of space and aren't just a house, but a home. When people see a well-executed design on such a small scale, they see how it could work.

Most housing is designed for someone else so that it ensures resale value. Spec houses and apartments place a premium on maximizing profits and square footage over functionality and aesthetics. When you have well-designed space that is built for you, the space works for you and feels homey. When you have a boring beige box, it's no wonder that people don't feel inspired.

Herein lies the awesome power of tiny houses: They open people's eyes to an alternative way of life. Many people grow up, go to school, get a job, marry, buy a house, have kids, slave away for decades, and then retire. Many people don't question this life path. They may not be aware of any other options, and it's sometimes sad to see them struggle to be happy on this path. The tiny house movement at least makes people aware that there are alternatives—even if they don't want to live in a tiny house, perhaps it will inspire them to think outside the box in other ways. They have been exposed to the possibility that their path isn't predetermined for them. It makes them start asking questions that they would have never asked. Finally it gives them the permission and confidence to make changes in their own lives to seek creative solutions to living better.

When it comes to how many tiny houses are actually being built, that is a tougher question. We do have a lot of anecdotal evidence and then good quantitative data, but the true number of tiny houses being built in the United States is somewhat a mystery. Various classifications, definitions, and legal paradigms obscure the accounting of tiny houses. It is also because tiny houses often try not to draw much attention to avoid scrutiny, while others are tucked away in remote corners of the world in off-the-grid situations. All of this makes it difficult to determine an accurate count.

If we look at the data that we do have, we can make some pretty strong inferences that the movement is growing, and with it, more and more tiny houses are being built. The primary source from which we gather data to make these determinations is the Web. Across the board, all major tiny house websites have seen traffic steadily climbing over the past few years.

If we look at Google's data for keyword search trends, we can see how the prevalence of the phrase "tiny house" is steadily growing over time.

We have also seen a steady rise of tiny houses being documented in detail on blogs. People building tiny houses may start a blog to describe or remember or catalog their building process. Reviewing current lists of known tiny house building blogs, there are well over two hundred in existence.

To make some solid assumptions, we have seen over time that there are more people building than those who are blogging about it. So, with over two hundred known tiny house blogs, it's safe to estimate that there are five to ten times that number of people who are actually picking up a hammer. This is a personal observation made from countless e-mails and personal interactions at events, home tours, etc. Again, it is difficult to truly account for all tiny houses; at this time we only have anecdotal evidence.

Another growth pattern that provides a good indication of the popularity of tiny houses is the number of resources and trainings that have become available to tiny house people. Over the past two years, we have seen numerous books, building guides, how-to's, and other resources hit the market to empower people to build their own tiny homes. So not only are there more tiny houses being built, but they are being built by better-informed builders.

Finally, we can draw some conclusions about how many tiny houses that are out there by not only the number of workshops, but the number of attendees. For example, as a guest speaker at one event, I was expecting to give a talk to thirty people or so. When I walked in the room and saw 120 people sitting there, I was blown away. The really interesting thing about this is that these are happening all over the place now, each with staggering numbers.

At each event, you find people who are dreaming about tiny houses;

then there are always quite a few who are there to learn right before they start building, and many even have already started building their tiny houses. There is also a good portion of the audience who will never build tiny houses, but dream about it. So as you get to know the people that at these events, you suddenly become aware that this isn't a blip anymore—it is truly a movement.

Obstacles and Possible Solutions

Every movement has its crosses to bear, and tiny houses are not alone in this. Luckily for us, it really is only a matter of time before we can break through most of these hurdles and gain acceptance in the mainstream.

The obvious and most difficult ones to overcome are land, loans, laws, and communities. Tiny houses exist in a legal gray area that can be a difficult place to reside. But, tiny house people want to be able to live in their homes legally, and municipalities have a vested interest in being able to regulate and tax tiny houses. This combination has the potential to bring about a lot of change because both sides are working toward a common goal.

The path to a legal tiny house that is accepted by municipalities is a difficult one. It will take time, money, and a lot of patience to achieve legal status, but in the end, the movement will begin to grow even faster! Just imagine a world where people say "no thank you" to the big banks, where they start paying for things with cash on hand instead of going into debt with credit. Imagine a world where fly-by-night home-building companies shrink away because their former customers are now building their own homes. Imagine communities where people are involved, engaged, and active citizens. Think of communities where the ideals of yesteryear have made a comeback, where neighbors act like neighbors, where modern-day equivalents of barn-raisings are a way of life. These are all things that
we can achieve when we pave the way for tiny
house communities that are legal, funded and brought to fruition.

It will take people working with their local city officials to show them the benefits of living small, how it will impact their communities and the people who live in them. It will take people setting up communities across the nation, providing examples to others to start discussions in their own town. Finally it will take a few good people to be living examples of what tiny living can do for the average person.

LAWS

The legal issue is a tricky one because of how the current system is set up. While many cities use the International Building Code (IBC), they often do so in a modified version. The convenience of the IBC is that a town can purchase these codes off the shelf, tweak them to their liking and then roll them out. It means a lot of time and money saved for them, and a code that has very few loopholes.

What makes this so tricky is that there are currently 3,144 formally recognized counties in the United States and they all have their own flavor of the code. What is more, the IBC rolls out a revised version of their code every few years, but they leave it up to the cities to adopt them on their own time line. Consequently, this means that some towns are running on the 2000 version of the IBC, while their neighboring county might be on the 2008 version.

The IBC itself is quite cumbersome and slow—sometimes new codes don't roll out for years. Right now they are already planning how to change the code as far out as a decade. So when you add up the decade of planning the IBC does, and then the familiar story of towns being sometimes a decade behind, we are looking sometimes at two decades to have any updates made to the code.

So what is the answer to this? I think we need to take a page from the RV industry and start establishing our own self-imposed code. The code that they use is quite simplistic and borrows a lot from other industries, but it still brings legitimacy to their industry and has drastically improved safety standards.

Some tiny house proponents will say, "Why don't we just become RVs and be done with it?" The answer is pretty complex. The cost to become an RV manufacturer is quite expensive, and then if your tiny house is labeled as an RV, you become tied to the legal frameworks that exist already. This could be good in some ways, but in most municipalities being labeled an RV is more of a hindrance than anything. With RVs come a lot of rules about where you can park, how you can park, and how long you can stay in your RV. An RV is typically defined as a motorized vehicle that is designed for temporary or seasonal living.

This is why I think the most practical solution is to institute a self-imposed code, generate sample language for municipalities to adopt, and become an American National Standards Institute (ANSI) standard. These things will do a lot to further the cause of tiny houses and pave the way to tiny house communities.

LAND

The question of land is also a tricky one. With populations growing, we are beginning to see land prices rise drastically and lot sizes shrink in size. Numerous reports indicate that worldwide we are going to have to centralize our living into houses in urban centers in the next one hundred years. While this is true for many parts of the world, it is somewhat less of an urgent matter here in the United States. When we read these reports, we need to consider the fact that almost half of the world's population resides in India and China alone: These areas are increasingly becoming urban centers, and density is skyrocketing. While there are some large cities in the United States, they pale in comparison to places like Mumbai.

Here in the United States, we have a lot of land that is largely undeveloped, and the density is very low. There is still cause for us to consolidate into more densely packed areas due to efficiencies with resources and other advantages. While we Americans may know this intuitively, there are many of us who want room to roam. Whether we shift to urban centers or better-designed townships, we are going to have to rethink housing. We should take lessons learned from tiny houses and apply them to higher-density housing.

Land today in the more popular locales is still quite expensive. In the past few generations, land has not been a commodity that is handed down to subsequent generations. Instead, people sell the land for a place in the city or because they don't want to work the land like their parents did. Parents dream of seeing their children succeed beyond their own accomplishments in life, but that often means that we give up the farm for a small lot in the city; we trade knowing the land for a college degree and
toiling behind a plow for a cubicle in a high-rise.

While some of us wish for the good old days, it is worth noting that we have achieved a quality of life for most of our citizens that is the envy of the world. While the United States is far from perfect, being a U.S. citizen has many advantages in terms of life expectancy, education, and access to food and clean water that many other countries don't have.

There have been a few models proposed for how to start a tiny house community. These tackle the issue of land, and then also streamline the legal issues. The added benefit of a community like this is that it can pool resources for things like common use outdoor spaces, community-owned solar arrays, shared vehicles, and a community common house in which people can connect and congregate.

Because the group is acting as a single buyer, they can purchase larger parcels than they would have otherwise been able to afford. It also means those with limited finances can still afford land but benefit from the community spaces and have a place to park their tiny house.

The benefits of these types of communities are great. They have been pioneered in the form of the co-housing model. The co-housing concept originated in Denmark and was brought to the United States in the early 1980s. The concept is a community that is composed of private homes that are supplemented by shared facilities. The community is planned and common areas are owned and managed by the residents themselves—while still maintaining private households, finances, and so on.

Another reason a tiny house community can really progress the cause from a legal perspective is because municipalities are far more likely to consider the interests of a well-organized group that is ready to develop unused land into a taxable community. Even if tiny houses only call for a small amount of taxation, cities see them as places where they can highlight good works for affordable housing, green communities, and other civic-minded causes.

The Smith Cabin by Charles Finn

The Smith Cabin by Charles Finn.

Photos courtesy of Charles Finn.

The Smith Cabin being moved to its final resting place for its new owners.

Towing the Smith Cabin.

How to Join the Movement

- Connect with local tiny house enthusiasts.
- Research how others are handling tiny houses in their cities.
- Develop a proposal for how tiny houses could be developed in your city.
- Talk with local officials about the benefits and examples of tiny houses.
- Participate in online and offline conversations surrounding tiny houses.

LOANS

It is an odd twist that I'm talking about home loans when it comes to tiny houses because it does seem to contradict most of what I have said up until this point. This is something that a lot of the people in the community seem to struggle with—and I include myself among them. The question comes down to: Are loans intrinsically bad, or are they merely executed badly by the profiteering big banks?

At this point, most banks will not lend to people for tiny houses because tiny houses currently aren't seen as having a market value. Banks need to know that if the loan goes into foreclosure, they can still get their money back. Right now tiny houses don't hold that kind of sway in the market so banks are hesitant to give loans on them.

Some people have used other collateral to take out a loan, and others have had some success getting personal loans for their tiny houses, but often the interest is quite high. Some people have financed tiny houses on credit cards, but I can't think of a worse idea because annual percentage rates on credit cards are so high—sometimes as much as 35 percent! So credit cards are a bad idea no matter how you look at it.

If there is any hope of a loan being offered on a tiny house, I feel the best option is one executed by tiny house people themselves. It could be in a community-funding model or in a nonprofit that manages a fund that administers loans.

People fall on both sides of this, but we have seen some models, like the Grameen Bank or Kiva—programs that connect people in developing and third- world nations with micro loans—that have shown that carefully issuing credit can have a big impact on people's lives. While these examples have found success in third-world nations, the values seem to translate well to this situation.

We can take some of the lessons learned and exemplified in these new models of social justice banking and apply them to loans for tiny houses. In an ideal world a tiny house home loan would be managed by a nonprofit entity whose mission is to provide access to credit in an ethical manner. The mission should never be making a profit, but to provide a service to its clients.

In the pursuit of this ideal mission, the nonprofit bank should be able to charge a modest fixed rate of interest because it will help ensure the organization's ability to serve people in the future and expand the number of loans it can offer. The execution of these loans should be made highly accessible and understandable to the common person, without the need of lawyers, in the form of terms of agreement.

The good news about loans for tiny houses is that many people can pay them off very quickly because they are small amounts, and also due to the fact that the tiny house that results from the loan will replace their largest expense (rent or mortgage). If a loan is made for a tiny house for the materials only, assuming the person will be doing most of his own work (many tiny houses take this route), then we can safely say that a tiny house can be built, on the high end, for $25,000.

If we design the loan so that payments start six months after the loan is taken, this gives people the ability to build their house and move into it before they have to make their first payment. Once they have moved into it they aren't paying rent anymore, so they can then turn that money toward quickly paying down the loan.

Consider that the average rent is $804 a month (according to the American Community Survey) and the average electricity bill is $103 a month (U.S. Energy Information Administration). Once you add in the remaining utilities, you are looking at around $1,000 a month spent on housing. Consider putting that toward a tiny house payment instead. If an expensive tiny house is $25,000, it can probably be paid off in about two years. It starts to become quite palatable when you compare that to the average car loan term, which currently is hovering around sixty-three months.

So, there are two big things to realize here: Since the tiny house is replacing our largest expense, we can tackle the debt very quickly. And it would take a lot longer trying to save up that amount on top of paying rent. So if the movement were able to execute an ethical tiny house loan program, it would most likely do well because of these two factors.

Building Codes for Tiny Houses

Dealing with building codes is another questionable area in the evolution of tiny houses, but most tiny house advocates have come to realize that it is the next logical progression. This is particularly the case if we want to come out into the light and make strides to become widely accepted and legalized in municipalities. In the end, many think that we will eventually be brought into the fold from a building codes perspective. The question then is, are we going to let them determine the codes for us or are we going to establish our own and create a precedent?

The codes we create don't have to be overly complex or all encompassing. As mentioned before, the RV industry has gone down a similar path, and their codes are quite basic. There is no reason for the building codes for tiny houses to be complicated. And there are some things that we can do to improve the quality of tiny houses through the use of codes.

Tiny house codes could actually be used as a resource for people to learn key techniques to build safer tiny houses. How this would be implemented would still need to be developed, but the code should be seen as a tool to empower tiny house builders, not limit them.

While there are quite a few parts of the IBC that are designed to maximize taxation and help the construction industry, the tiny house code should purely focus on making tiny houses safe. The tiny house community could develop the codes and it would be up to the tiny house builder to follow them.

Overall, tiny house advocates do have some hurdles to overcome in order to progress the movement, but there are a lot of options for us to pursue. We are fortunate that we can draw inspiration from other industries. It won't be easy: These changes will take the dedication of many in an organized and thoughtful way, but I believe it is doable, and in our lifetimes. We talk about intentional living a lot when it comes to tiny houses; we must also be intentional in our actions to enact some of these measures.

Typical Tiny House Utility Bills Per Month

Water $6
Electricity $25
Propane $20

Deb Delman and Kol Peterson of Caravan—The Tiny House Hotel

Photo courtesy of Deb Delman and Kol Peterson of Caravan—The Tiny House Hotel.

How It All Started

Deb has lived in a lot of "funky" places over the years and Kol has done a lot of work with accessory dwelling units in the Portland area. So when they saw a vacant lot in a popular area of the city, they knew there was potential. Tiny houses were something that they had been drawn to through their years of living in different spaces, but for them a small house was more their speed. Kol first came upon tiny houses when he took a workshop because he was attracted to the efficient use of space in such a small house.

Kol later met Deb, and together they envisioned the first tiny hotel. After years of working with the local code officials they were able to come to a solution. It was touch and go at times to get the houses through the system, but eventually they prevailed with the help of many people in the government who became personally invested in seeing it come to fruition.

Deb and Kol eventually ended up with something akin to a campground built on a commercial lot, which was allowed for use as a hotel. It's a combination that would make any inspector's head spin. Many times they had to adjust plans as the inspectors required different things; sometimes it seemed almost arbitrarily. But, after a lot of work, it finally came to be.

Caravan—The Tiny House Hotel is new to the tiny house scene, but it has made quite a splash. The hotel is comprised of several tiny houses situated on a converted urban lot in the heart of Portland, Oregon. Each tiny house has its own design aesthetic. The Rosebud is a cozy mountain cabin; The Pearl is "modern minimalist" and focused on being very energy efficient; and The Tandem is a Portland style that is a little funky.

Beyond being an interesting concept, the hotel has also brought about a sense of community. The Caravan has a great outdoor space where people simply come to hang out. It is a bit different than your traditional hotel; here there is a lot of interaction between the hotel guests. People enjoy the outdoor room created by the circling of the houses, along with comfy chairs, a fire pit, games and great company.

Photos courtesy of Deb Delman and Kol Peterson of Caravan—The Tiny House Hotel.

Photos courtesy of Deb Delman and Kol Peterson of Caravan—The Tiny House Hotel.

The Houses That Make Up Caravan—Tiny House Hotel

The houses at Caravan are a little different than your standard tiny house. With very basic kitchens and actual flush toilets that are connected to the grid, these houses are designed more to suit hotel guests than full-time residents. In each house the kitchen is very small and features just a microwave, a mini-fridge, and a hot plate. That is because the hotel is located in a trendy restaurant district and most people coming to stay want to eat out.

In terms of storage, the houses are built to accommodate luggage and a few items, but not much else. This gives the houses a bit bigger feeling because they don't have to contain everything a person needs to live. Each house was built by a different person and is leased to Caravan to rent out. This allows Caravan to rotate out the houses later on and provide some variety while builders can showcase their tiny homes to potential customers.

Of the current houses at Caravan, The Tandem is the largest at 160 square feet. It features two beds—one daybed on the main floor and a lofted bed with a normal mattress. The house was designed by Eli Spevak of Orange Splot.

The Rosebud is a more traditional tiny house style built to have a cozy cabin feel. It is 100 square feet and features an all-wood interior. The house was designed and built by Hal McClendon and was the first thing he ever built. The house features a lofted bed for two and a built-in couch with storage.

Finally, The Pearl stands out from the rest as being very modern looking, with the metal roofing extending down the sides of the house. The other ends are covered in a dark wood siding that also has a modern feel to it. The inside can sleep two people, one in a loft and the other in a daybed seating area on the main floor—all packed into 100 square feet. The Pearl was built by Shelter Wise.

Caravan allows people to spend the night in a tiny house and try out tiny living for themselves. The response has been phenomenal. Reading the comments from the guest book of people who realize tiny living might be for them is inspiring for Deb and Kol. They aren't the only ones in the area that are taking to tiny houses. Deb and Kol told me that within a few miles there are already ten people living in tiny houses and another twenty people that they know of personally who are building.

Photos courtesy of Deb Delman and Kol Peterson of Caravan—The Tiny House Hotel.

Bringing About Change

Deb and Kol think that tiny houses have a place in bringing about change in housing for a broad range of people. Deb sees tiny houses impacting people who want to live a simpler life, but they are also a practical solution to homelessness. Caravan is a unique showcase of tiny houses that allows people to learn about them, be exposed to a community of tiny houses, and even try them out. It exposes the general public to tiny houses in an innovative way.

The interior of Caravan's The Tandem tiny home, designed by Eli Spevak of Orange Splot.

Tips From Deb and Kol

- Tiny houses hold potential not only as a home but as a business, too.
- If you are not sure about living in a tiny house, try staying in a tiny house hotel first to try it out.
- Outdoor spaces are key to tiny houses. They can increase your

usable space and help you build community bonds.

Photos courtesy of Deb Delman and Kol Peterson of Caravan—The Tiny House Hotel.

The interior of Caravan's The Tandem tiny home, designed by Eli Spevak of Orange Splot.

The interior of Caravan's The Rosebud tiny home, designed and built by Hal McClendon.

Photos courtesy of Deb Delman and Kol Peterson of Caravan—The Tiny House Hotel.

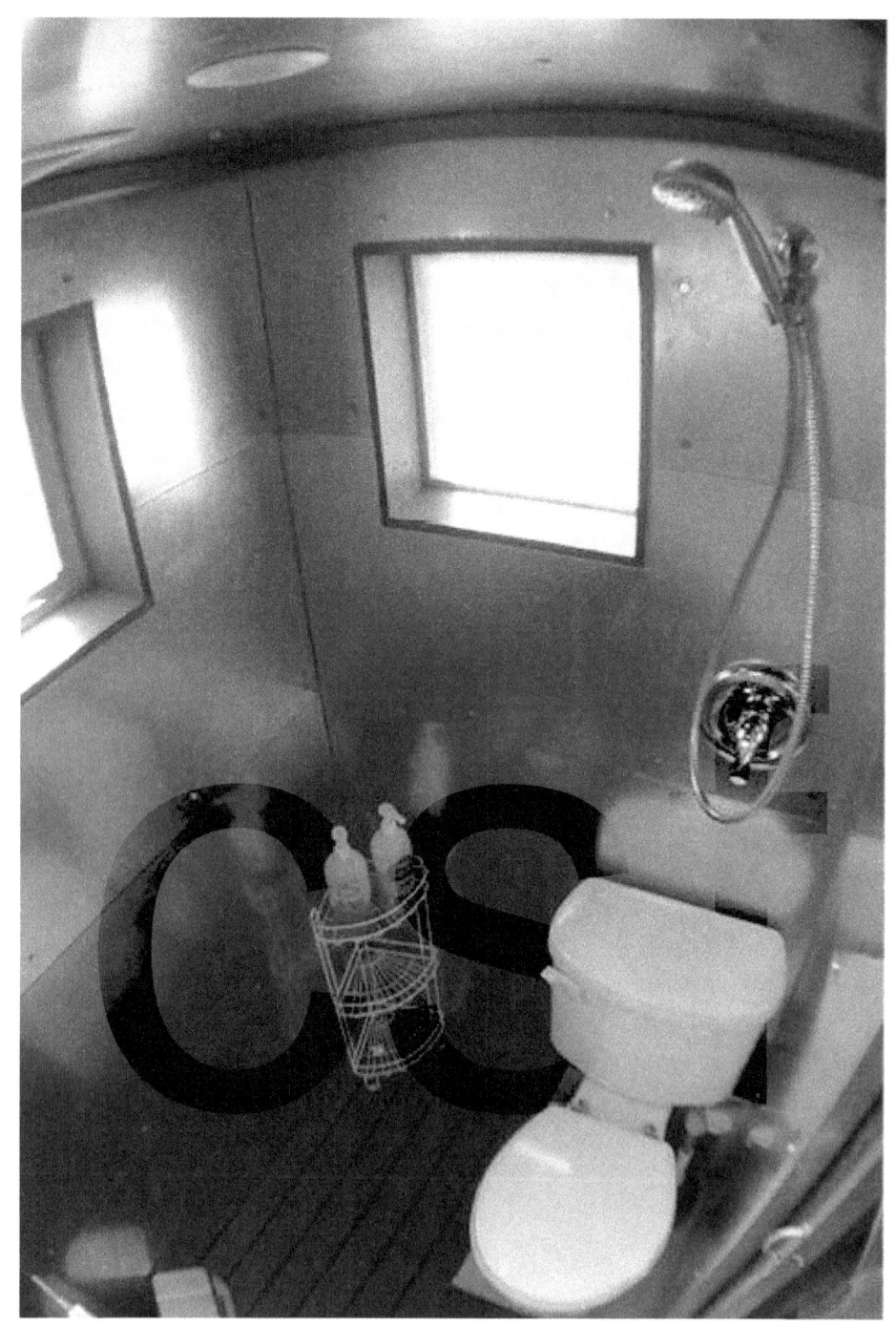

The interior of Caravan's The Pearl tiny home, build by Shelter Wise.

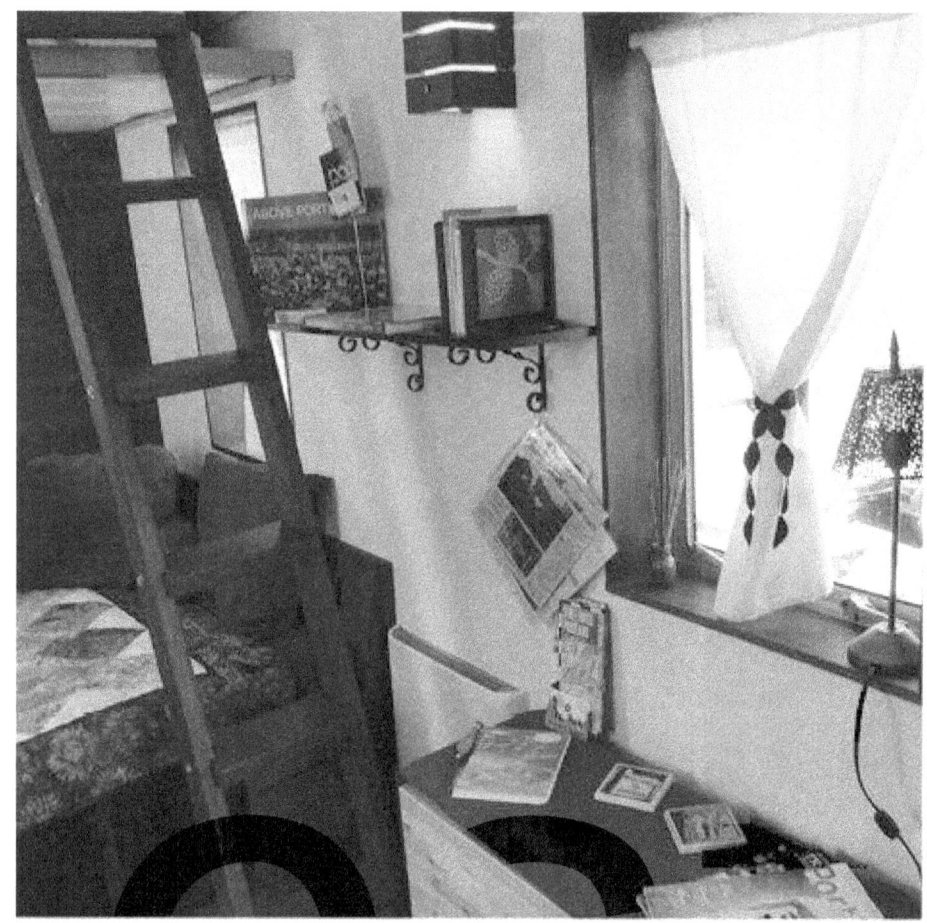
Photo courtesy of Deb Delman and Kol Peterson of Caravan—The Tiny House Hotel.

Photos courtesy of Dan Louche, tinyhomebuilders.com.

HOW CONSUMER CULTURE IMPACTS THE MOVEMENT

I have talked a lot about consuming and marketing to this point, but there are some aspects of this that need special attention because they help frame our thoughts on the shift to living life tiny. Understanding and recognizing these concepts is sometimes half the battle, because you may not even be aware of the influence they have on your behavior.

Case Study: Dan Louche and Kathy Truhn

Photo courtesy of Dan Louche, tinyhomebuilders.com.

How It All Started

When Dan's mother, Kathy, needed a new place to live, they considered many options, but none seemed quite right until he came upon tiny houses. Without telling her, Dan bought a trailer and began to build the tiny house. That Christmas, Kathy came to visit; pulling into the driveway they saw this little house that was there. Kathy thought that Dan was building a little cabin to spend time in the mountains—but she was in for a surprise.

"Dan showed me around," Kathy said. "When I walked in I said, 'Oh my God, this looks so much bigger on the inside than you would have thought from the outside.' And looking around inside I could see so much potential for his cabin that I thought was going to be so cool. Then Dan said, 'There is just one other thing … I'm building this for you, Mom.'"

Kathy was ecstatic. She loved her new home as Dan showed her where all the parts of the house would be, how it was laid out. They talked about where she could put her things, how she wanted a futon on the main floor so she could entertain friends and then sleep without having to climb into the loft.

Dan didn't want to tell his mother until the house was at a point where she could begin to see what the house would look like. He knew if he told her ahead of time it would be a much harder sell, so he waited until it was almost done to show her.

Working on the house in his driveway, Dan tried to get the house done quickly so his mother could live in it. But after four months of building the house in plain sight of the road, his Homeowners' Association issued a letter that he must remove the house within eight days. So they got the house to a point where it was road-worthy, then headed south.

When Dan brought the tiny house to his mother's place, he had most of the basics done. There was a bathroom, plumbing, and electricity. From there, Kathy determined where she wanted her kitchen, her futon, and her living room. Dan had finished most of the interior paneling but left the cabinets and the flooring up to his mother, who hired someone locally to finish the last parts of the project. Kathy soon moved into the house and began living tiny.

Adjusting to Living Tiny

Even though Kathy has never been one to have a lot of things, she did find that the tiny house took some getting used to. She had to pare down some of her clothes, but she said that the clothing she gave up was clothing that she wore infrequently.

When Kathy has guests over she makes up the futon and turns her bedroom into a living room. There she and her friends can have coffee, talk, watch TV, and enjoy each other's company just like any other house. "It's no different than any other house that is 5,000 square feet because I'm only in one room, wherever I'm at," she said. "It's not much more than anyone needs."

The only difference for Kathy is the money. She can do all that she needs to do in her home, without a mortgage and with very low bills. Her power bill tops out at $25 a month and water is about $12—not because she uses that much, but because that's the minimum charge to keep the service on. Beyond that she uses a tank of propane a month, which runs her $18. Overall, her monthly costs to live are small, but she feels that she isn't giving up anything in the process. Since she is retired, it is very important to keep her living expenses low and it means that she can do much more, like visit her grandchildren more, go out to eat with her friends more, focus on her hobbies, and simply not have to worry about the bills as much.

Tiny living has brought about many positive changes in her relationships. For the first time she has had the money and the time to visit her grandson for his birthday. As a couple, Kathy and her husband find the space very suitable for them. In a small space "you don't argue as much, because where are you going to go?" she said. "You make amends really quickly." Living with her husband has brought them closer because "if you don't live with your best friend, you're going to be in trouble quickly."

Kathy told me about her friends who all have much larger homes, some several thousand square feet. Her friends lament to her about all the cleaning they have to do and how it's getting harder to move about in such a big house as they age. "It's a simple way of life, but it is a very rewarding way of life," Kathy said. "There are lots of things I can do other than looking after the house."

In the beginning, Kathy's friends were of the mentality that it was good for her, but not for them, that it could never work for them. But as time goes on Kathy has seen her friends start to shift in thinking as they see her living a very happy life in her tiny home. Now Kathy hears all the time from her friends that they wish they too could live in a tiny house just like hers. When I asked her what stops her friends from making the transition to tiny living, she said, "It's because they don't know what to do with all their stuff that they spent their whole lives trying to pay for. They are so inclined to having stuff that it's scary for them to think of paring down."

When I asked Kathy about how she has adjusted to living in a tiny house, she told me how it happens every time she is in a store. "When you are looking at that vase or that pillow and you think, 'Where I am going to put this?' you don't have the space for it so you put it back on that shelf. It comes down to—is this thing something that I love, does this thing make me want to get rid of something that I already have in order to have it in my home?"

So Kathy makes decisions every day about what is in her house and what isn't. It is an intentionality that most don't have, but which her tiny house brings to her life. Once she has a place for something, that's where it stays. "There's not a lot of space to be moving things around," she said, "so when you take something out, it goes back right away."

In the small space she said she is constantly caught up. You don't have the space for a mess, and because of its size she can clean the kitchen quickly as she walks from the bathroom to her couch. Cleaning the whole house takes no time at all for her. Even deep cleanings might take only thirty minutes of her time, while most of the time it's a matter of only minutes.

Photos courtesy of Dan Louche, tinyhomebuilders.com.

Photos courtesy of Dan Louche, tinyhomebuilders.com.

Photo courtesy of Dan Louche, tinyhomebuilders.com.

Building Codes and Zoning

As Kathy continued to live in her tiny house, they have had several building inspectors come out and look at her home. The saving grace of her setup is that there happens to be a traditional house on the same property and the city has yet to be able to prove that Kathy doesn't live in that house. After the initial round of inspectors, the situation has calmed down quite a bit, so now the city has moved on to other things, leaving

Kathy to live in her tiny house as she sees fit. They see it as a small act of civil disobedience, in the form of living in a tiny house.

Layout Considerations

When designing the layout of the tiny house, Kathy knew she didn't want to climb up into a loft at her age. She opted for a futon, and there was only one wall that could accommodate that width. With the futon's position selected, they then turned to the location of the bathroom. They decided to put it on the other end of the house. From there most of the house laid itself out. They knew they had to have the door on one of the sides, and then the kitchen's location became obvious.

Kathy told me how she essentially had a mental inventory of everything in her old house's kitchen and what things she wanted to bring into the space. From there it was a matter of designing the cabinet layouts of her house to fit all those things.

In her kitchen, Kathy can do almost anything she could do in a traditional kitchen. She has a toaster oven for baking, an induction burner for cooking, a microwave, and a small fridge. It's all that she needs to cook for herself or even guests. The largest group she has entertained was "six adults, one child, and two dogs"—all fitting comfortably in her tiny house.

Growth of the Tiny House Movement

Dan now also builds tiny houses for other people. As he sees it, there are two groups of growth of the tiny house movement. There are those who are attracted to simple living and the lifestyle, but maybe not in the form of a tiny house; then there are those who are interested in the movement because they want to live in tiny houses themselves.

The dream of simplifying their lives is a major draw. "There are so many people who are overwhelmed with their day-to-day work to pay their mortgages," Dan said. He has had many people describe their situation where they had everything pre-defined for them. "You go to school, you graduate, then you go to college, then it's time to get a real job, which leads you to think about getting a house and having kids," Dan said. "Even though there isn't someone standing beside you telling you what to do, it ends up happening, and sometimes that path leads people to a place where it's overwhelming or not something they want."

So it is no wonder that for those of us who feel like we had a life that we might not have chosen, or one that doesn't quite fit us, the simple life is appealing. Dan has found that this life has a universal appeal for many of these reasons.

Dan sees three main barriers to tiny houses: financing, insurance and, most importantly, places to put tiny houses. As the movement grows, he hopes to see these issues being tackled as more and more people live in tiny houses.

With tiny houses being artificially limited by these restrictions of building codes, zoning, financing, and insurance, the market can only go so far. Taking on these challenges will lead to massive real growth for tiny houses, both for the people who want to live in them and for businesses wanting to support them.

Dan thinks the next big thing for tiny houses will be the development of tiny house communities. It is a particularly difficult concept to execute, but building a community would address both the need for land and the barriers to laws. From there the tiny house community could be a launching point for other communities and could pave the way for others to find legal solutions to tiny housing in their own community.

Tips From Dan and Kathy

- Consider where you'll want to be in your retirement years. Tiny houses are perfect for retirees, whether they want to travel or stay

close to family.
- The time and effort spent cleaning a tiny kitchen and tiny house is minimal, which is valuable not only for an aging population, but for everyone.
- Not all tiny houses have to have a lofted bed; consider a futon or a Murphy bed.

Keeping Up With the Joneses

There is something about our culture where many of us feel the need to demonstrate that we have wealth, power, fame, and other qualities that many don't have. It is a dreadful game of who can outdo whom when it comes to houses, cars, clothes, and so much more. How we got this way, I don't know, but it enters us into a game that we will never win. Except for a few people on this earth, there will always be someone richer, someone more powerful, or someone with better status than us.

It is a sad state of affairs when you seek to be better than someone else because of your material things. There is no shame in wanting a good life, to live comfortably, to enjoy the things you own, but when these desires overtake you, they can bring you to a place that is not admirable. The idea that you are "better" than someone else because of the items you possess—or that you need to own more items to keep up with your peers—is dangerous.

Symbols of Happiness

Very closely related to keeping up with your neighbors is the plight you face when you invest in things that are symbols of happiness, but don't actually bring you enjoyment. While there is a thrill in buying an item, this often wears off and you are left back where you started with the credit card bill in hand.

Symbols of happiness are things that you believe bring you joy, but often are just placeholders for what you truly want. This is a tricky thing for even the most experienced tiny house dweller because in some ways it is human nature. A great example of this is many people have photos of tropical scenes as their desktop at work. While you are locked up in your office at a job you don't like, you have this photo of some place you'd rather be.

Things such as a white sands beach are symbols of our happiness. What might seem to be a harmless desktop image can actually create internal turmoil for you at a subconscious level. While it can be hard to realize, these things can weigh on you because you are sitting at a stuffy desk rather than on a beautiful beach. You feel like you are missing out.

So when it comes to the symbols of happiness, you need to be cognizant of them. If they are within your reach, you should actively pursue them. For those that you honestly admit aren't achievable in your lifetime—perhaps swimming in a pool of thousand dollar bills—you need to process and come to terms with those things.

The point is when you have things in your life or in your tiny house that represent something that you want to be, they should be used for motivation to achieve that goal. If they aren't realistic, then you should come to terms with it. So even if today you are in a terrible job in a dull gray cubicle, make a plan to achieve your dream. At the very least, a day spent in that cubicle isn't drudgery; it is a day spent working toward that goal.

The 100 Things Challenge

One interesting outcome of the tiny house movement is what many of us call "The 100 Things Challenge," which, simply stated, is a challenge to own only one hundred items. People might accept the challenge in their quest to reduce material possessions. I personally think this is a bit extreme because those who pursue this school of thought count every little thing. For example, if you have a fork, knife, and spoon to eat with, they count as three things; a few pens, each one item; each pair of underwear, an item each. So we can see how quickly these things can add up, including just basic necessities.

What I like about the 100 Things Challenge is that it is a pretty straightforward approach—and even if you don't pare down to one hundred things, having a goal is a very strong motivator. The 100 Things Challenge's principles are:

- Reduce. By reducing the number of our possessions for an extended period of time, we prove to ourselves that consumerism does not define us.
- Refuse. By refusing to go along with the misleading lifestyle of consumerism, we form new priorities in line with personal virtue and what is best for the world around us.
- Rejigger. By rejiggering our lives through simplicity, we nurture better relationships with family, community, and nature.

What these principles seek to define is an alternative to how you normally lead your life. While only owning one hundred items is pretty extreme, understanding that you can reduce the amount of possessions gives you room to prioritize other things in your life, such as relationships.

What stands out in this paradigm is that it firmly points out that part of the process is refusing to go along with others. When you say "no" to certain things, it means you can say "yes" to others. This is the prioritization of what is important. This intentionality can be a powerful force in your life.

Finally, the 100 Things Challenge uses the term "rejigger," but what I think is the takeaway here is that you are thinking about your life and your possessions from a broader perspective. You are taking a look at the whole system and understanding the dynamics that are in play. By taking the long view, you are able to make calculated decisions that can have big impacts on your life.

Much like when you examined your expenses and determined housing is the largest sink of money, you must think strategically about your life in general. That is what the people from the 100 Things Challenge are getting at when they say "rejigger." Instead of making small, incremental changes, you need to take a step back and assess where you can make the largest impact with a change.

The goal is to find where you can make a change that will result in the largest amount of progress toward your goal. Much like the novel approach to housing that tiny houses bring as a solution, you must be prepared to really push the limits and make creative changes in your life to achieve maximum effect.

How to Reduce Your Possessions

Getting rid of stuff can be very hard to do, but it is a necessary part of tiny living. The simple reality is in a tiny house, you don't have a lot of space. I have talked at length about the shift in your thinking that needs to occur first, but now it is time for the rubber to meet the road.

Even those who don't have a lot of stuff often have a lot that they simply don't ever use. For example, I heard an interesting fact: Most people don't wear 80 percent of the clothes in their closet; most of us tend to stick to the same 20 percent. While this isn't true for everyone, I would suspect that it is the case for most of us. This can easily be applied to most of our possessions.

There are a few techniques that I recommend in my one-on-one consultations with clients that have proven to be quite useful. While some of these techniques work better for some people than others, usually we can see progress with most of them.

DON'T TURN TO STORAGE SOLUTIONS

When people have a lot of stuff and it becomes a problem, often they don't seek to reduce the amount of stuff they own, but instead to better organize it. This is a trapping that we all fall into, but it isn't the right approach. The question should not be, "How can I organize my stuff?" It should be, "How can I reduce the amount of stuff I have?"

Truth be told, there is a lot of money to be made in storage solutions, but not a lot of money being made in the simplification of things. So there are tons of storage solutions at the store, on television, or on the Internet to organize your things. But be wary of falling for that trap. It isn't that these things aren't useful or shouldn't be used by tiny house people—I encourage you to do so—but to think that you can fix your problem by just organizing better will get you nowhere.

So take an inventory of what you really need, using the methods below, then utilize space-saving options. This will make for a much better execution of these storage solutions, save you money, and save space, too.

The Box Method

I discovered this method when I moved into an apartment as a short-term place to live before I finished my tiny house. Since I wasn't going to be there that long, I packed most of my things up in boxes that never were opened on purpose. I unpacked the bare essentials because I didn't think it made sense to unpack everything. What I realized was that after six months, all those other boxes were still sealed up. I didn't have to go into them once in six months!

It made me wonder if I really needed those things. If I didn't need any of those things in a six-month period, what was the likelihood that I'd need them in a year, two years, and so on? Almost everything in those boxes became fair game to be reduced.

The trick with this method is not to cheat. I'd also suggest breaking up your living space into smaller subsets for you to tackle one at a time. This might be my favorite method for reducing stuff because it helps you really home in on what you use and what you don't use. It also helps you evaluate things to make practical decisions. Its simplicity is almost comical, but elegant. It truly resonates with the tiny movement.

To start, find a box or multiple boxes that are size appropriate for the stuff in a certain area of your life. The important thing to remember is to tackle one defined area at a time; usually you can define an area by its function. Your desk is a great place to start because it is usually very cluttered and doesn't have a lot of sentimental items in it. Later on, you can move on to your clothes, then the kitchen, and so on.

Take everything—and I mean everything!—out of and off of your desk and box it up. You may want to cheat and leave out a pencil or note pad, but don't. Make sure every drawer is empty. Make sure the desktop is clear along with the floor. Once you have done this, write today's date on it and take this box and put it under your desk or within arm's reach.

As you begin to work and find that you need things, go to the box and pull out that one single item. If you need a pen, get one pen, not all of them. If you need a ruler, take only it out of the box. Continue doing this for a month from the date you wrote on the box. At the end of the month, schedule twenty minutes in your calendar to sort through the remains.

During this twenty minutes, set your trash can right next to your box and begin considering each item. My prediction is that 95 percent of all the things in that box you will end up throwing away, donating, or freecycling. You may decide that an item is only used occasionally, but you really need it. Ask yourself:

- Is this something I could borrow easily when the need arises?
- Is there another object that can do this function?
- Is there an item that could achieve the same thing in a smaller form?
- Could I achieve the function of this item in another way?

For many items, you will find that you can borrow them or you don't really need them.

Then there are those things that you just have to have. Your emergency inhaler is a good example. However, the snow globe that Deborah in accounting gave you four years ago and that has been sitting in the back of a drawer is not. Perhaps if you only use a three-hole punch once or twice a year, you can borrow one from a friend.

Depending on the things you are sorting through, you might have two piles: throw away or donate. The bulk of what is left in the box you will get rid of, and in the end you will have an area that is cleaner and has the things you need, not just what you think you needed.

The Three Piles Method

The three piles are "keep," "throw away," and "donate." Like the box method, you should try to tackle small, defined areas because it will let you make serious headway and give you the feeling of progress. These smaller divisions also help you stay motivated because if you say you are going to do the whole house, it isn't likely you can achieve that in a single day. At most, each area should take an hour or two to sort through.

I find this method works well for clothes, because I can quickly make decisions on things and there isn't a lot of sentimentality to clothes in most cases.

The trick with this is staging the three piles and then making your decisions quickly. In most cases, if you think about an item too much, you will talk yourself into keeping it and the things you want to really keep are often very obvious to you.

Before you start the sorting, it is a good thing to think about what standards you are going to evaluate things on. What criteria will you use to judge what stays and what goes? What clothing fits your lifestyle? What is comfortable? What looks good? What fits well? What is in good repair? Set these parameters without thinking about any particular item. If at the end of the sorting you find you have a much larger keep pile than the rest of them, consider tightening your standards and go through the pile again.

When I do this, I usually use my bed for the keep items and then designate two areas on the floor for the trash and donate piles. This helps make sure you don't accidentally throw away the wrong things if the piles start to grow into each other. Another way could be to remove everything from your closet and hang up the items you wish to keep.

Remember, the key here is to make decisions very quickly and impulsively. If you don't truly love it and use it often, you probably shouldn't keep the item. I have a pretty easy time with clothing because often the clothes in my hamper are the clothes that I wear 90 percent of the time, while things that are hung up or put into drawers I haven't touched in a while.

> *"I want to be intentional about my freedom—in choosing it, honoring it, and protecting it. One of the best feelings I know is feeling truly free."*
> —**KRISTIN ARMSTRONG**

Eric Bricker

Photo by Joseph Pettyjohn, courtesy of Eric Bricker.

This tiny house built by Eric Bricker in Austin, Texas, features an open living space that connects to an outdoor sitting area. The custom countertop (pictured at right) is from a company called Reclaimed Spaces.

Photo by Joseph Pettyjohn, courtesy of Eric Bricker.

A sliding reclaimed barn door leading to the bathroom. Next page, the kitchen features a hanging plate rack and storage.

Photo by Joseph Pettyjohn, courtesy of Eric Bricker.

One In, One Out

This is more of a maintenance strategy, but I wanted to mention it because it will help you to determine what you really want to keep and what needs to go. The premise is simple: If you want to bring a single item into your house, you must choose a like item to remove. I recommend this strategy for people who are new to living tiny or have been battling too much stuff in their tiny house.

The value here is that you are making decisions on what is more important to you, what has more value. The intentionality of the decision and the act is key. As you go through this process, you will end up with a collection of items that you value more and more, because you are constantly refining and re-evaluating each thing.

The result of all this organization and minimizing is hopefully a set of things that you find very useful, very valuable, very beautiful, and highly sentimental. Just imagine if you could honestly say, "Everything in my home I love, down to the pen I write my shopping list with."

Christopher Carson Smith and Merete Mueller

Photo courtesy of Christopher Carson Smith and Merete Mueller of the movie *Tiny: A Story About Living Small*

How It All Started

The land came first and the tiny house came soon after. Merete tells the story of how Christopher had a moment when he was coming to grips about turning thirty. Trying to balance the realities of adult life and where he had wanted to be by the time he turned thirty was something he struggled with. He and Merete were big travelers, but having a place to come home to was important for them. Christopher had always dreamed of coming home to a mountain cabin.

One day Christopher found himself up in the mountains. Later that night when he came home, Merete asked him about his time in the mountains and he responded, "I may have put an offer down on some land." For Christopher, this was a very impulsive decision—even for him, a person who usually doesn't plan too far in advance. Faced with turning thirty, he had made the decision on the spot that it was time to stop putting off his dream.

For the longest time it was always "when I have money or when I'm older," but he realized that later was too long to wait. Once he had the land purchased he looked into building a small cabin on a foundation, but his cabin design was too small to meet minimum house sizes and codes. Christopher went back to the drawing board and came to tiny houses.

The first tiny house they had seen was Dee Williams' tiny house on the cover of a magazine. At the time there weren't a lot of tiny houses out there for them to learn from or draw inspiration from so they did what they could and learned along the way.

Most of the design came out of a few key things that Christopher wanted to incorporate and materials he found along the way. This process of design by discovery worked out well for them as they built their tiny house, the first thing they had ever built.

Construction of the house was a trial by fire. As Merete tells it, "Christopher looked up at the house and said to me, 'I need to put a roof on.' Then I remember him looking up on the Web how to build a roof. I remember him reading blogs and watching YouTube videos every night trying to learn what to do for the next day."

Not only were Christopher and Merete learning about the building process, but they were also filming it along the way. It started out with them filming the construction of their house, but quickly grew into a full movie. They turned it into the film *Tiny: A Story About Living Small*.

Photo courtesy of Christopher Carson Smith and Merete Mueller of the movie *Tiny: A Story About Living Small*

Living Simply

The land that Christopher had bought was about a two-hour drive outside of Boulder, Colorado, and very remote. The entire house was built to be off the grid, with solar panels and a basic water system. Time spent in the house is a simple way of life.

It also highlighted how much people take for granted when they turn on their faucet or flip a switch. "In terms of a place being livable, you can't underestimate how important running water is, even if you are conserving it," Christopher said. The one major change they made since building their tiny house was installing a plumbing system. Initially they would just carry in water, but after living like that for a while they realized it was a convenience they wanted.

Even after the upgrade, a lot of their house is still very simple; they don't have complex systems like most houses do. The simple lifestyle of living in a tiny house might seem tedious to many people, but to Merete, "living that way is very grounding." And that is what they like about the lifestyle, a simpler way away from the chaos of modern life.

After they finished their build, they began to see other tiny houses with dormers. While they like the loft for sleeping, they think it would be neat to add dormers to the house. Since building they have seen "people really push the paradigm of tiny houses," Merete said, so they are attracted to a wide array of new ideas. If they were to have another house they might try a more modern design with a main floor bed instead of a loft.

All in all, their house has exactly what they need to live in it. It is so much more than just a place that they happen to live in. "There are so many stories in the house, even before we moved into it," Merete said. That fact surprised both of them quite a bit. Living in different places over the years, they never experienced anything like that. "What that taught me was that is what it takes to build a life, it's the experiences that form it," Merete said. They don't see material things as bad, but when something doesn't have meaning, it is just disposable or clutter that doesn't add to their lives.

Christopher never was one to have a lot of stuff, but the change made him think more about the stuff he did have. The things that he owned brought more meaning to him and he was aware of the impact on his life, too.

Even things like cooking dinner, which many people would normally rush through, they now spend more time on and enjoy more. The time in the house is a slower pace than the rest of the world; it's "nice peaceful hangout time."

Photos courtesy of Christopher Carson Smith and Merete Mueller of the movie *Tiny: A Story About Living Small*

Building Codes and Zoning

When they first moved into the house, they got a lot of media attention, which brought their home under the scrutiny of building inspectors. A week later, Christopher received a letter asking him about the toilet in their house and telling him that he had to have a driveway installed. After calling the municipal powers that be, he was able to explain how he handled the toilet and said he was "camping" on the land. "At first I thought the driveway was pretty silly, but it was a simple thing to do and then I had an address and an easy way to find me," he said. So Christopher had a small driveway installed that leads to nowhere essentially. His tiny house sits farther into the property and he only had to pave a few feet to meet the code.

How Life Changed for Christopher and Merete

After moving into the house they were able to save money to travel more. While they were filming and showing their movie, they always knew that they had a place to go back to. That was a big deal when Christopher decided to leave his job to focus on the film. He realized that he could leave his job and it wouldn't be the end of the world because he had a home to live in. Since it was off the grid, he didn't have to worry about rent, a mortgage, or utilities. That was an empowering thing for him. It also made him sleep better at night knowing that he always will have a home, regardless of his work situation.

Merete decided to pursue a new career opportunity where she could leave behind her old job, which was a scary experience for her. "If all else fails and things go horribly wrong, I can just come back to the tiny house," she said. "It makes the risk so much less."

The one thing that Christopher does have to contend with is his student loans. When I asked him about how he would feel if he also had a monthly mortgage payment, he said, "I couldn't imagine if I had a mortgage." He is looking forward to spending time in his house and quickly paying off his student loans and never having to worry about debt again. With these changes, they began to shape their lives in the form that they had only dreamed about.

Photo courtesy of Christopher Carson Smith and Merete Mueller of the movie *Tiny: A Story About Living Small*

Tiny—The Movie

Christopher and Merete found themselves in a community of tiny house people that were taking the same journey. "One of the things that we have been really inspired by is the community in general," Merete said. "The whole community has such a DIY-type of ethic. It's not just people building their houses, it's people building their lives in really unconventional and creative ways." In that creative change they began to see that, while they were building their own houses, they were also building their lives.

This community was apparent in every city that they visited to show their film at festivals and showings. Every time they came to a new city, they met people who were really excited about tiny houses and a surprising number of people who were building their own tiny houses. "We met an executive who came up to us in a very expensive suit and admitted that he kept a file of tiny house designs for his own tiny house," Christopher said.

These experiences happened in most cities they went to. "Tiny houses appeal to us on the most basic of levels," Merete said. "It's a life that inspires."

Christopher told me about how many of the people who come to his screenings are there by chance, because they had tickets to the film festival, not because they had ever heard of tiny houses. "It's interesting when these people watch the film and, even though they had never heard of tiny houses, at the end they just get it," he said.

Therein lies the power of tiny houses. "A lot of people don't even realize there are other options than the life that was laid out for them," Christopher said. "Then this whole new world is opened up for them. Realistically, tiny houses aren't for everyone, but hopefully they can realize a way to live that is applicable to the life they want to live."

The inspiration that they see in their tours around the United States has made them realize that it isn't just a few people building tiny houses; it has grown into a movement. When they first started building, they were one of a few. Now they see new tiny houses every week. There are more builders, more blogs, more resources, and more interest every day.

Back when they started their film, they had been worried that they might not finish it before the tiny house thing got "old." "But it doesn't seem like it's getting old," Christopher said. "It just keeps growing." They have seen more and more evidence of the growth. "Part of it is the aesthetics, the look, the feel of tiny houses," Christopher said, "but really it's that people are waking up to the reality that we can't keep going on in the same type of lifestyle with over seven billion people on this planet."

So, while Christopher and Merete don't think tiny houses are for the vast majority of people, they do think houses in the 400-square-foot size that are well designed, beautifully crafted, and well laid out are the wave of the future. Christopher pointed out that right now your options are "a small apartment that is soul-less or a tiny house on wheels to get around the building codes." Merete responded: "The real story here, the story that is more threatening to mainstream culture, is not tiny, but small. The conversation is starting to shift. Now we are talking about building codes and lifestyles. Sometimes you need an extreme to shift things back to reasonability."

It is opening the conversation not about tiny, but about small that Christopher and Merete think is the real impact here. It has the potential to change the culture, to wake people up, to subvert consumer culture and leave Wall Street reeling.

Photo courtesy of Christopher Carson Smith and Merete Mueller of the movie *Tiny: A Story About Living Small*

Tips From Christopher and Merete

- Sometimes problems will arise with local codes or authority. It's best to be flexible and think creatively, and solutions are nearly always possible.

- Feel free to deviate from your initial plans if you find something is not working. For example, Christopher and Merete decided they really did want plumbing, so they installed it.
- You can spend a lot of time planning, but there are times when you just need to go for it.

Photo courtesy of Mark Walters Photography.

THE PATH TO LIVING TINY

For many people, the path to living in a tiny house is typically a process. At first, they may simply be curious, having been brought to the concept by some driving force in their lives. Or they are seeking a remedy to something that they wish to improve upon. It could be the escape of debt and a terrible job; they may want to be more environmentally responsible; or they just want to live a simpler life. Whatever the reason, the decision to pursue a tiny lifestyle is often a gradual one.

Despite what we wish to believe, humans are creatures of habit—we desire to maintain equilibrium in our lives. So we typically approach drastic changes in our lives with caution. When you face the challenge of making a major change, it is cause for pause and reflection. This is important, because the shift to tiny living is a significant one and deserves thorough consideration.

There are many forces that might dissuade you from taking these steps; they range from tangible things—building codes, for example—to societal pressures, your family, and your friends. No matter how much planning you have done, there will always be things that test your resolve. It is inevitable. You cannot avoid these things, so here is a list of some common roadblocks you might encounter as you plan your tiny life. Hopefully this knowledge will help you navigate the ins and outs of planning your tiny house.

Building Code Tips

- Talk with local code enforcement before you build.
- Understand the difference between primary and secondary residences.
- Look up local minimum habitable dwelling requirements.

- Partner with a contractor; they will know the rules and the players.

Building Codes and Red Tape

Legal governance and municipal bureaucracy sometimes cause a series of hurdles that people encounter when building a tiny house. This is one of the more tangible roadblocks that we face. Municipalities and governments seek to control things in their jurisdiction in order to maintain order, ensure public safety, and levy taxes.

Their primary vehicles to do this—as it applies to tiny houses—is through building codes, zoning, and inspections. When it comes to regulating building on a city level, it behooves a city to standardize regulations because it can more efficiently categorize, legislate, and tax structures. The current paradigm utilizes building codes to define what a structure is and how it should be assembled.

The issue with tiny houses is that they do not fit the paradigm that building codes have set out. They are often too small to meet the minimum requirements for a dwelling, and there are other issues with being classified as an RV or mobile home. Bureaucracy establishes itself by first fitting each thing it must deal with into a certain box. That box then defines the path through the red tape jungle. This works very well for governments because they can say you must fit in one of their boxes, one of their definitions. But tiny houses don't fit well into a certain box.

Local municipalities are enabled to enforce these limitations and rules by issuing fines, condemning structures, and blocking access to utilities. These roadblocks can seriously discourage a tiny house dreamer from becoming a tiny house dweller, but there are creative solutions out there. One good reference is an e-book I wrote called *Cracking the Code* (available at thetinylife.com) that reviews the issues surrounding building codes and zoning for tiny houses and explains how to approach them.

Social Pressure

Another barrier to overcome is social pressure. The thing about social pressure is you often don't even realize it is impacting your behavior and thinking.

To illustrate the effects of social pressure, consider being in an elevator. The old TV show *Candid Camera* put unsuspecting people in situations that were out of the norm, filmed their reactions, and presented them for comedic entertainment. One entertaining clip had several secret actors enter an elevator with an unsuspecting person. Instead of walking in and turning around to face the door (as people usually do), the secret actors walked in and faced the back of the elevator. The poor person not in on the gag would almost instantly turn to face the back of the elevator with the rest of them. There was even a clip where the actors would turn to face a different direction and the person would follow. The unsuspecting person did this because he felt it was the norm, because that was how the other people were acting.

While this is a simple—and somewhat silly—example, it demonstrates that we have been trained by certain societal norms. Norms are ingrained in us, even if we don't realize it. In this case, the unsuspecting person obviously felt very uncomfortable with not conforming to the group.

When you apply this concept to tiny houses, you begin to see how wanting to live in a small house might have some social implications. Expectations from family, friends, loved ones, and coworkers will be something you have to face when looking to move into a tiny house. People may question you extensively about why you want to live in a small space; they may want to give you gifts even though you don't have the space for such items; and they may form wrong impressions of you based on assumptions they make about your lifestyle.

In the end, you will need to come to terms with these pressures and gain the support of those whose opinions you really care about. You will get used to explaining your house and why you live in it, and you will develop a narrative that allows others to at least gain some understanding of the life you live. The reactions will be varied: Some just will never understand it, but overwhelmingly, people find it fascinating that you live in a tiny house.

Although these are just a few obstacles we must cope with, in the end we achieve tiny living because we came to it with a purpose, we are driven, and we see value in it. In the following section, I outline several steps you will need to take to make your way to tiny living.

Kate Jeffreys

Photo courtesy of Kate Jeffreys.

Simple cabin in Hana, Maui, by Kate Jeffreys.

Photo courtesy of Kate Jeffreys.

Mosquito netting over Kate's bed.

The front porch of Kate's jungle cabin.

Needs vs. Wants

Living in a tiny house is much more than simply selling all your belongings and moving into your house. It is a process of change that you go through with your thinking and your approach to life. Making the move to living tiny requires a process of self-examination and understanding your needs. In order to be able to live in a tiny house you must go through these steps to make it a successful endeavor. The biggest thing about living in tiny houses isn't the house, but the life you lead in it.

Living in a tiny house, the simple fact is that you don't have a lot of space for yourself and for your stuff. Because of the limited space you must begin to reduce your possessions. For many, this is a welcome task because they have seen how clutter can affect us negatively and the true cost that comes with it (time and money spent acquiring the stuff, caring for the stuff, organizing the stuff, housing the stuff, being stressed by the stuff). However, this is often a difficult process for many—even those who live in small spaces—because our culture has instilled a perceived need for more and more stuff.

It can be a rewarding experience because you are able to home in on what is very important to you, what has function, and what is just blocking you from the life you wish to lead.

As you have come to understand that there are lots of social norms and influences that determine your behavior, so is the case when it comes to determining your needs and your wants. This is difficult for us today because our society often uses the words "need" and "deserve" rather cavalierly. You may find yourself saying, "I need that new shirt" or "I need that new car." It's a cultural quirk that often serves as justification for buying more and more stuff. There are very few things you truly need in your day-to-day life. Understanding that even just using this vernacular triggers a consumer mentality is an important step when it comes to what you consume.

An important part of this self-examination is to understand how marketing and advertising impact your buying habits. Ads often influence quite subtly, and they can lead you to want the product—they may even lead you to make an impulse buy at the store. As you begin to understand these facets you will catch yourself—I do all the time: I'll be in the store and see something I don't need, but I still consider buying it. It is there where I realize I'm falling into the consumer trap, one elegantly laid out by marketers but nonetheless present. When I recognize this, I can avoid the purchase. If it is something I really think I'd like, I will often say to myself that I can get it next time I'm in the store. Quite often, I never seek that product out again, even though I might be in that store regularly.

> *"Have nothing in your house that you do not know to be useful, or believe to be beautiful."*
> —**WILLIAM MORRIS**

SENTIMENTAL ITEMS

Since there is a limited amount of space in tiny houses, you must limit items to those with a very strong value to you. They tend to be useful to you, often in multiple ways. With each item, you must be intentional about owning it, using it, and storing it. Without this intentionality, it's easy to fall into the trap of too much stuff.

When working with people new to the concept of tiny houses, I have often used this old exercise:

You wake up from a deep sleep to find your home on fire. You jump out of bed and through the window you see your loved ones safely outside beckoning you to escape the flames. You have but one moment to grab a single item before fleeing to safety. What do you grab?

It's an unpleasant scenario, but it makes you think about the things that are very important to you and what things might be negotiable. Try this exercise when you think about what you will create a place for in your tiny home.

We often don't have a use for certain sentimental items. This is where many people get caught up in keeping too many things. Emotional attachments can be very strong. You need to realize that sometimes items don't really have true value to you. In addition, you might have dozens of items that remind you of the same thing. This is where living in a tiny house can be difficult. Many people have to dig deep to understand that attachment we have to sentimental things. If, after examination, you decide you really want to keep a special sentimental item, and there is room for it, that is fine. There are no hard-and-fast rules when it comes to tiny houses.

This is the main point of understanding needs vs. wants: We need to be intentional about the items we own and keep in our houses. Some people might be quick to judge, seeing tiny houses as a deprecation of quality of life, but it isn't that at all. We choose to live this way and the things we choose to do without are intentional and thoughtful, and the lack of material goods helps us achieve something else we want. The key word here is "choose." Empowered with choices and the freedom to make them, we aren't limited by many rules or restrictions.

Determining Your Needs

Examining your needs versus your wants helps you to define what is essential to daily life. So let's do that first, and from there we can begin to find the form and function of your tiny life in a tiny house.

The best place to start is to imagine a typical day in your life. What do you do? You get up, have a bite to eat, shower, dress, and go off to work. You come home and then maybe eat some dinner with a spouse, significant other, or roommate. After dinner you clean up and then quickly pay some bills before you retire to a cozy chair to read a book.

Whatever your day is like, think about the things you require to accomplish your daily activities. Remember, living in a tiny house is not living without; it is living with exactly what you need and just that. Make a list of these things to see some of your needs.

For example, when you get up, you need to make breakfast, so you'll need a space to make the food. For those of you who don't cook much but tend to have simple foods and eat out, you don't need a big space to cook. In fact, there are small spaces in cities that only keep a microwave and a mini fridge; they don't even have a kitchen because they can eat out so easily. For those of you who love to cook elaborate meals, you might want to have a well-appointed kitchen.

It's important to understand the context of the need so you can later design your tiny house to meet that need. This is where a list is useful, as a tool to capture all your needs so you can keep them in mind when designing later.

Evaluating Your Day-to-Day Life

Take some time to write about your usual daily routine. List your usual tasks, routines, and schedules. Add time estimates if you wish.

_____
_____
_____
_____
_____
_____
_____
_____
_____
_____
_____

Take some time to list items that you think will be essential to day-to-day life.

_____
_____
_____
_____
_____
_____
_____
_____
_____

Choosing Plans

- Do the plans include framing, electrical, and plumbing?
- Is the trailer that the plans are based on available to purchase?
- Do the plans include a detailed materials list?
- Does the seller provide support if you have questions?
- How much will it cost to have alterations made?

Find plans at thetinylife.com/plans.

THE PITFALLS OF WASTED SPACE

Part of the reason large homes have so much wasted space is because our houses are often designed for others; because we are concerned about resale; and because we add in spaces and functions for what I call "outlier" activities.

This is best exemplified by guest rooms and formal dining rooms. Both are types of rooms that most modern large houses have, and at the same time they are so seldom used. It is here where we fall into the trap of being concerned about our home's resale value and the outlier activities.

Common outlier spaces include:

- guest bedroom
- living room
- formal dining room
- rooms to "grow into"

Outlier activities are those things that you do very seldom. In the case of a guest bedroom, unless you have guests staying with you every weekend, why have a whole room for the few nights a year someone visits you? When you determine your needs, it's important to distinguish between everyday activities and outlier activities. If there is an outlier that you really want to incorporate, consider other creative solutions.

For example, if you have guests only a few nights a year, consider having a futon that you can dress up with nice linens, or even put your guests up in a hotel. My favorite solution is to suggest, "Instead of coming here, let's all go to the mountains or the beach. Let's make it a trip." So you can see, there are quite a few solutions to consider. It just takes some creative thinking.

THE PITFALLS OF RESALE VALUE

When it comes to building your tiny house, plan on not being able to resell it. If you are able to—down the line—great. If not, no harm. It is a relatively small investment anyway. The best piece of advice I received when building my tiny house was to build it for me, for my needs, and for my life. This is important because it is such a small space; it really needs to be custom-built to suit your needs. To have it any other way is really going to hamper your life in the tiny home and the impact will be significant.

A way many tiny houses are customized is through our hobbies and careers. More and more people are working from home. And there may be storage needs for the items you need to do your hobby; you may even do the hobby in the home. Consider your needs in these areas carefully and remember to seek out creative solutions in order to save space. For example, you can find another space in which to do your hobby. If you love to play tennis, consider joining a tennis club where the locker room lets you keep your equipment in your locker. If you work from home, consider using coffee shops or co-working spaces to meet the needs of your professional career instead of jamming it all into your tiny house.

Another really great resource to consider when determining your needs is the book *A Pattern Language* by Christopher Alexander. In this book, Alexander visits hundreds of homes across many cultures and countries to determine a universal set of needs that a home serves. It's an interesting study of the true needs of humans because it considers many types of lifestyles and bridges cultural gaps.

Developing a Plan

After you have fully explored your needs, it is time to use them to determine the design. I see lots of people who love a certain house plan or certain look but neglect to consider how their needs will be met—or won't be met—by that house. It is for these reasons I have people first identify their needs, and then determine the design. The adage "form follows function" couldn't be any truer than in a tiny house.

When you are figuring out what your tiny house is going to look like, it is important to consider the needs it must meet, but also how it will meet them.

If you need a place to keep your professional work clothes and your casual clothes, consider how much of a wardrobe you will really need; from there you can understand the size and capacity of your closet. You might also realize that you have a summer wardrobe and a winter wardrobe. Instead of having a closet for it all, many tiny house people swap out their winter and summer clothing and pack away the rest in a less accessible space, cutting their closet in half.

Once you have your expanded list of needs and how to achieve them, consider the space that is required. Now you can begin to play with storage options and how they will work and look in your tiny home.

At this stage you can begin sketching floor plans and outlining where things will go. While I am a fan of computer-aided drawing programs like SketchUp (a free 3-D design program), sometimes I find that the tactile quality of pencil to paper brings about more ideas. At this point, don't worry about straight lines, erase marks, and moving things around. The process will be messy; it will require tons of revisions and you'll go through dozens of designs before settling on something.

If you plan to use someone else's design, consider how they designed the storage, the allocation of space for certain parts. For instance, if their design has a huge, well-appointed kitchen and you don't cook, you can still use the design but size it for your needs. Usually what people like about other people's designs is the exterior look of the house. It is also an attractive option for first-time builders because the detailed plans help them get their feet wet with home building.

Realize that the bulk of the plans will get you to a shell of a house, and then some direction on how to finish it, but once you get to the interior finish work, you take over the design for the most part. In most cases this is intentional because the designers realize that a house is so personal to the owner that you'll want to modify the interior design anyway.

Once you begin to get comfortable with a layout and design, the next important step is to map out your tiny house to scale. Get some masking tape and map out your design on a floor somewhere to the same size as the house. Then, consider what furniture, if any, you are going to add. Once you do this, begin to act out your day in the tiny house. You'll quickly realize that there are some things that just don't make sense and you'll want to change them.

When considering the design and layout of your tiny home, be sure to explore other resources for design ideas, storage options, and other elements. These can be online, in magazines, or in books—but be careful to not get caught up in neat ideas that don't meet your needs.

Developing a plan for your tiny space can be time consuming, but it is a very important step to building your tiny home. It ensures that your tiny house will meet the needs of your life.

Layout Considerations

When you are planning your layout, consider questions such as these:

- When you open a door, where will it swing?
- What clearances will the door need?
- Where will your clothes be stored?

- Where will dirty clothes be stored?
- Where will you store your food?
- Where will you store your cooking utensils and pots and pans?
- Where will the trash go?
- Do you want an additional space for recyclables?
- Where will you eat in the house?
- Will you need a table?
- Do you eat watching television or at your desk?

All the minutia of your life matters here, and while you might feel ridiculous playing house inside your taped tiny home, it will help you immensely in the long run.

Seeking Out Experts

Many people who wish to live in a tiny house come to the building process with no building experience, but they would like to build it themselves. So when we pair the desire to build your own tiny house with first-time home builders, you can see there is disconnect between the desire and the skill.

While some people have construction skills, seeking out experts in the building of tiny homes is often a good and necessary step for people of all skill levels. The process of building a house is no easy task. Even with training there is a lot to learn, and you will spend hours researching different aspects of the building process. There are several resources out there, but the three most common approaches are through workshops, e-books, and one-on-one consultation.

WORKSHOPS

In recent years we have seen a rise in tiny house workshops aimed at equipping people with the skills to build their own homes. Most of these are single-weekend workshops that aim to give people the confidence to take that first step toward building their tiny homes. For a long time workshops were only presentations, but recently there has been a trend toward more hands-on experience. These hands-on experiences have given people a big leap forward in their building knowledge and confidence, enabling them to learn some core home-building skills.

E-BOOKS

People often also purchase a book or e-book, or check one out from the library, to guide them in their tiny home building project. These can range from plans to instructional books. While these are good resources, there are some out there that are lacking in depth and breadth. A few stand out, and you should research carefully.

ONE-ON-ONE CONSULTATIONS

Even with an intensive hands-on workshop, you can only learn so much. Many people really do need additional help and a place to go to get questions answered. This is where one-on-one consultations really shine. A great resource is Tiny House Craftsman (www.tinyhousecraftsman.com). They help tiny house people gain the skills and knowledge they need in one-on-one sessions.

Joining online discussions and perusing websites are also helpful. You will gain a wealth of advice from people who have already created their tiny homes. You may even be able to connect with people in your area and see their tiny homes in person.

Some people have a really good friend or family member who is willing to help build, and that is an invaluable resource. This is an approach that many tiny home builders have used because, frankly, there wasn't any other option. For a long time, tiny home building was a pretty solitary activity. It was a new movement and the first people building tiny houses were pioneers. With the movement growing as it has, we have seen a rise in tiny house construction blogs, where people document their process of building for others. Sometimes the later steps on these blogs are sparse because as people get deeper into their build, they focus more on the building than the blogging.

The next evolution of tiny home building support has come to the forefront—professional help, where people who have already built tiny homes will work with people building their house for a fee. This could be an in-person consultation if they are located close to each other, or it could be via Skype or on the phone.

The ability for people to pick up the phone and give their personal tiny house expert a call is a real leap forward, because it can keep the building process moving, ensure things are done correctly, and give first-time builders confidence in what they are doing. Going forward, I expect to see more services like Tiny House Craftsman begin to crop up in support of the first-time home builder.

Though most people don't possess the skills to build a tiny house at first, there are several pathways to achieve the goal. When building your own tiny home, you should tap into resources that allow you to be supported during your build.

Finding Community

One of the most interesting things I have noticed when doing interviews for this book is that even though the people I talked to live far apart, lead totally different lives, and are drastically different types of people, they shared some distinct commonalities. I discovered that they all said that living in a tiny house made them engage a lot more in their community.

When you live in a tiny house, you live in such a small space that you have to get out in the world to do your living in places other than your home. When you live in a house the size of a large parking space, you don't have room for absolutely everything. This leads you to find creative ways to meet those needs outside the home. In the tiny house world this is called outsourcing. In the context of tiny houses, outsourcing means you are seeking the support and services of the space around you.

Outsourcing and community connections are key elements to the tiny life, and it means that you must become a more active participant in your community. The word "participant" is a carefully chosen word here because it implies that you are not only using the resources of your community, but you are giving back at the same time.

This could take a variety of forms, from using the services of a local business, catching the game at a local bar with your friends, using your public library to borrow books, or having dinner parties at friends' houses. However this manifests itself, it means that you are investing in those connections and relationships that might have been there as matters of convenience, but now are integral to your life.

Common things that people seek out in their local community are places to do laundry, get an Internet connection, use space to conduct business, attend larger events with people, and perform leisure activities. Many people who live in tiny houses also work in their tiny home. Using co-working spaces, rented meeting rooms, community centers, coffee shops, and other spaces is often necessary to meet the various demands of your business.

Whatever the needs of your lifestyle require of you, understand that engaging the community around you is an important aspect of living in a tiny house, more so than with traditional housing. Developing connections with the people in your community and enjoying the spaces that it has to offer are great rewards to this life.

Contending With the 3 Ls

On the path to living tiny, there are several steps you must take before the first board is ever put in place. This is quite intentional because it gives you the foundation on which you can gain your footing to have the construction of your tiny home be successful. After talking with lots of people who have built their own tiny houses, I've noticed a specific process that has emerged as a common denominator for everyone. This process will make things go more smoothly, help you avoid pitfalls, and create success.

The last stage before actually picking up your hammer is to contend with what I call "the 3 Ls:" land, laws, and loans. I covered these in chapter three, but we'll revisit them because these three things are the biggest barriers to living in tiny homes, and you must at least consider them before starting.

LAND

Having land is a huge asset when it comes to living the tiny life. It's something that a lot of us don't have, or the land we do have will not suit the need. Though the physical space required by a tiny house isn't large, many people seek a larger parcel of land to have space to do other things like grow a garden, provide vehicle parking, or create a community, or simply to be surrounded by nature.

Many people want to live off the grid or in a homestead style, which inherently means they need more space for their energy production, water sources, food production, and gray/black water solutions. In many cases, this means several acres of land.

LAWS

When having to contend with laws such as building codes and zoning laws, many opt to "fly under the radar," so they need a larger parcel of land in which to conceal their home and give them a measure of privacy. Ultimately we hope to find a path to a legal solution for tiny houses, where we can be taxpaying citizens living within the law.

As I mentioned earlier in this chapter, the powers that be are sometimes not as accepting of newer ideas when it comes to building codes and zoning. These entities rely on being able to classify and process things quickly, all of which are contrary to what tiny houses are and need. In order to work with your local code enforcement, it requires knowing the codes, being creative, and often getting variances issued for your tiny home.

In my experience, most code enforcement officials are interested and intrigued by tiny houses, but at the same time they have a professional duty. It's their job, so they need to adhere to the rules.

Working in your favor is that you are coming to them proactively seeking a solution. Also, having a good attitude and the fact that the home you are building is attractive will help. These three things are something that building inspectors don't see very often because people often try to skirt the law and have bad attitudes when they get caught. The biggest offenders are usually those with less than honorable intentions.

So my suggestion is to approach the process by learning everything about the code, then come to them with an attitude of, "I want to do this the right way and want to work toward a positive outcome with you." Working with them, you can often find a good solution when it comes to tiny houses.

LOANS

The final "L" is loans. Most banks will not give loans for tiny houses because they are a nontraditional home. In their eyes it has little-to-no resale value, which means the loan doesn't have an asset to take in the event of a default. It can be very difficult to get a loan from a bank. That means you need to save up to pay for the house with cash.

In many ways, the fact that you can't get a loan on a tiny house is a good thing. It keeps you truer to some of the values of the movement. In other ways it does present an issue when it comes to accessibility. The simple fact is that these homes still represent a sum of money that many people don't have.

Someone could spend ten years saving up, but if they could get a loan, the amount could be paid off fairly quickly when they no longer need to pay rent. In this scenario, a person would be looking at paying off their tiny home in one to two years—money that would have been spent on rent. The difference in years spent living instead of saving can have some very large impacts on that person's quality of life.

I generally don't recommend getting a loan from friends or family. When a loan is made between you and friends or family, it changes the dynamic of that relationship.

What was once based on mutual respect, love, and friendship now suddenly has a new aspect driven into it: monthly payments.

Disagreements over money are the largest cause of divorce; this fact would most certainly translate to the breakdown of relationships over money. It's sad that money can be such a divisive issue, but we know it to be true. So, if you do enter into an arrangement such as this, be wary of the dynamics it brings.

Ways to Engage Your Community

- Patronize local businesses.
- Volunteer to help others.
- Use local services: libraries, public transportation, etc.
- Work outside the house even if you "work from home."
- Have guests over, but outside the tiny house.
- Have a great outdoor space.

Noel Higgins

Photos courtesy of Noel Higgins / Teach Nollaig.

The simple kitchen in Noel's tiny house features open shelving.

Noel's water heater uses the heat of the chimney to warm his water tank.

Photos courtesy of Noel Higgins / Teach Nollaig.

The wood-fire stove in Noel's tiny house.

Building It Yourself vs. Hiring Someone

Many people start out knowing that they either want to build a tiny house themselves or have someone else build it for them. For whatever the reason, most just know what is right for them. However, there are some things to consider when weighing your options.

The biggest factor is money. In traditional home building, labor accounts for 50 to 60 percent of the overall cost to build a home. It's something that people don't realize is so expensive because the materials costs are often obscured intentionally by a variety of tactics.

There is an interesting dynamic in tiny houses because most people know the actual cost of the materials that go into a house. Even if it is just a ballpark figure, they often have access to the material cost of a tiny house within a few thousand dollars. This plays an interesting role when it comes to having someone build it for you, because while a professional tiny home builder still charges the same labor costs, it's often transparent what those costs are.

The question then is, "Are you willing to pay double the amount so someone else will build it for you?" For some, it is well worth the money and hassle; others decide to do it themselves.

While the cost of labor is expensive, it does bring some advantages. With a professional builder you have someone who is very familiar with the process. They bring a level of experience to the table that is rare and valuable. It often means that the quality is going to be better than what you might be able to achieve because they are more skilled and aren't learning as they go along.

Most tiny house builders are very small operations and many will critique their work, so it behooves them to do a very good job and deliver a quality product. They are repaid by word of mouth and recommendations. In a tight-knit community such as ours, word would spread fast of dishonest tiny house builders, so this works in your favor.

Beyond the fact that professional tiny house builders have more experience in building tiny houses, they can often provide great insight into the design process, in terms of how to maximize the space, creative use of materials, and working with you to achieve a design that complements your needs.

Finally, a builder will often be able to deliver a completed tiny house in a few short weeks or months. This is compared to most DIY home builders who take up to a year to build a tiny house because they are learning as they go along and often still working a full-time job.

For those who wish to build their own homes, it can offer a lot of advantages. Some people don't have a lot of money, but they may have time to spend on the project. If time is money, building it yourself is a good option if all you can afford is the materials. It is important for you to budget your time and understand how large of an investment in time it will be.

For the first-time home builder, it will require about five hundred hours for learning, researching, and securing materials, and then one thousand to fifteen hundred hours to actually build a new home.

Be prepared to face possible roadblocks on your journey. There will be times when you planned to work the whole weekend and you realize there is an issue that you need time to think about to come up with a solution. There is weather to deal with for those who don't have an indoor space to build in. You will get to a point where you need a particular material and the stores don't have it in stock, or don't have the right size or you can get it online much cheaper. All of these setbacks will eat up weekends you had planned on working through. But it's okay, because you should take your time with the building and understand that there is value in it because you are learning.

Managing the materials is going to be one of the biggest challenges you will face. It is knowing what type to buy, what to look for, and then managing the orders. It is a big time sink when you need to do special orders from any store, because sometimes it can take weeks for an item to come in.

These items also happen to be your biggest expenses and, as in the case of windows, the options can be staggering, so sometimes your decision-making process will hold you up. These times will vary depending on how close you live to the manufacturers and their stock on hand. Of course, we'd all like everything to be in stock, but the reality is that you will end up having to special order a lot of things.

There will even be some things that your plan calls for that you can't find where to purchase them. This is the case for many tiny house plans that call for specific items; for example, the Tumbleweed Fencl plans call for a 30"×30 shower stall. There isn't a manufacturer that makes such a thing, unless it's custom. This also happened with lumber on a few occasions; the particular species and sizes were very hard to find. It once took me two weeks to just find a place that sold a particular component.

So, as you can see, there will be several issues you will need to contend with as a DIY tiny house builder. In the process you will learn a lot about building, the materials, and the business as you navigate getting your materials. For those of you who opt to hire someone to build it, part of the cost of labor is their expertise on sourcing materials quickly.

Building Materials Wait Time

Average time for receiving items:

Windows	4–6 weeks
Roofing	3–4 weeks
Trailer	2–4 weeks
Flooring	1–2 weeks
Siding	1–2 weeks

OTHER ISSUES SURROUNDING TINY HOUSE CONSTRUCTION

When you are building your tiny house, you will run into problems that you never would have dreamed of. It's funny how a lot of what we thought would be the biggest problems doesn't even compare to some things that befall us in our quest to live tiny.

Invariably, things will always take way more time than you thought. That's just something you will have to realize and accept. Time will be taken up with an extra trip to the hardware store, the battery for your drill that you forgot at home, or having to take a moment to step back and think about how you are going to handle something. It all adds up, and it means you'll spend way more time doing what was on your list for that day.

There will be times when you need a second set of hands or friends to come out to help with the build. Company is very welcome, but it also means showing them how to do what needs to be done. So instead of building, you are teaching someone how to read an $\frac{1}{8}$ of an inch on a tape measure. Just like you were when you first started, your friends have never attempted anything like this before. They don't have the skill you now have. Just know that sometimes having help can come with extra baggage.

Weather is a big issue to contend with when it comes to the building process. I would have loved to have an indoor space to build my tiny home, but it wasn't in the cards. The clock starts ticking as soon as you seal up your insulation with subflooring. Even if you choose to use treated subflooring, it creates a large flat space for water to pool on, and that can cause issues even if you cover it. There will be times when you'll need to work quickly, and times when you'll have the leisure of working more slowly. Just keep in mind that you'll need to work around the weather patterns in your area.

Finally, the most important thing I tell people is to take their time with the process and enjoy it. The journey is part of the experience and you should savor it. For many of us, we have been dreaming about this for years, and for a dream to come to fruition is something that many don't get to enjoy. So take your time with it and if there is a day that you are at wit's end—and trust me, there will be those days—know that it's okay to take the rest of the day off and come back to it fresh.

Case Study: Macy Miller

Photos courtesy of Mark Walters Photography.

How It All Started

The first move was nerve-racking: Macy had spent the better part of a year and most of her savings building her tiny house, and now it was time to move it from where she had built the house to its final destination. Even though the location where she would live in her tiny house was only across town, there is always the fear of moving your tiny house for the first time. Luckily, Macy was too tired from getting ready for the move to worry as much as some tiny house owners.

Her house's design is a departure from the standard tiny house design. She describes the style as "modern and/or contemporary." Her house features a shed roof style that is actually designed to be a green roof—reclaimed pallet siding—and instead of the standard utility trailer, she found a gooseneck trailer that presented its own design challenges.

After considering many styles initially, she landed on this one because she felt that with tiny houses, less is more. But more importantly, "It's a machine for living; it reacts to how I function as a person," Macy said. From there she had her starting point for the design.

Photo courtesy of Mark Walters Photography.

Designing a Tiny Space

One advantage Macy had over some tiny house builders is that she not only built her own tiny house herself, but she is also a professional architect. Most of her projects at work are large buildings, but this tiny house gave her the opportunity to build a home. Since it was her first time building something of this size, and because she felt that the design aesthetic warranted cleaner lines, she wanted to "go back to the basics, to simplicity of structure."

Macy was excited to see how her design skills manifested in the real world. As she put it, she was "trained in design, not construction," but she has to make decisions every day that will impact people building the structures she creates on paper. So building her house allowed her to really grasp some of the issues that come up when trying to build—and that has made her a better designer.

Even now that her house is completed and she is living in it, most of her friends and coworkers have never seen her home. Having been fully absorbed in the building of her house for almost a year and a half, many things were put to the side as she tackled this project. She had never built anything like this, and even when she told her friends that she was building it herself, most would say that they "couldn't see me holding a hammer, let alone building a whole house," she said.

Being a Female Builder

There is an interesting trend in the tiny house movement that goes against many of the norms of our society—and that is that tiny houses are predominately built by women. In the building industry, female builders are almost unheard of, but with tiny houses, it's quite the opposite. I asked Macy for some insight on being a female builder.

She told me how she was used to operating in male-dominated fields; in architecture, women are in the vast minority. So when it came to building a home she didn't really think anything of it. She attributes some of it to the mentality of her generation. "At some point you have to be self-dependent," Macy said. "As a woman there are times you have to be able to stand up on your own."

Macy realized that the cost of housing was the biggest expense in her life, and that impacted how well she could be independent. Looking back she knows that "nothing about building a tiny house is hard—it just takes dedication, patience, and perseverance." In past generations, women typically looked to their male partners for security, but now she feels more comfortable knowing she is able to stand on her own two feet. She understood that "I needed to take care of myself" when it came to her basic needs.

Macy brought up how tiny houses impact men and women differently. Traditionally, the man is seen as the provider, which means he should have a big house. That big house is seen as a status symbol, a measure of his success. "It is seen as a brave thing for a woman to take on building a tiny house, while a man might be questioned because people think you can't afford a bigger house," Macy said.

Macy put all the preconceived notions of women builders aside and got to work on her home. Most of the work she did by herself, citing herself as a perfectionist and not being able to let others work with her as the reason. The house was a major learning experience for her; a lot of the process was researching the various steps of the build. The biggest challenge for her was the electrical work because it made her very nervous.

Photo courtesy of Mark Walters Photography.

Approaching the Build

Working with tools lent to her from her father, she learned how to slowly craft her house. Initially she used hand tools, and then, gaining confidence, shifted to more power tools, which helped speed up the process. "There was a fear factor as you learned the powerful tools," she said. "The table saw was my arch nemesis. In the beginning, I was terrified of it, but now I'll use that tool no problem." Macy said that now she has "more respect for the table saw than anything else."

Macy found a gooseneck trailer on craigslist. That type is different from many other tiny house trailers in that it is just a flat utility trailer. Prepping the trailer took a lot more time than she had anticipated. Prepping the steel for paint and insulating the interior space took her almost two months' worth of nights and weekends to complete. This was a big challenge for her because in the time that she had the most excitement and energy in the project, this stage consumed most of that energy for little visual results. During this step she did a lot of work that no one would ever see, but that was crucial to the integrity of the structure.

Looking back, Macy said if she had to do it all over again she wouldn't buy a used trailer. After all the time and effort that went into the trailer, plus the additional $600 she put into adding an axle and replacing the old ones, it cost her more in time and money than a new trailer might have.

Photo courtesy of Mark Walters Photography.

Building Codes and Zoning

The biggest challenge for Macy was not the building of a tiny house, but living in a tiny house. Her tiny house is not permissible by code because of its small size, so Macy sometimes worries about issues that might come up. Her house was built to code with the exception of the square footage. Codes in her area require that a house be a few more hundred square feet to be legal. In the end she feels that if something does come up, "it's just a question of coming up with a new solution" in terms of where to park it or how to work with local code enforcement.

That puts her in an interesting position because she actually serves on the building codes committee for her city. She hopes that she can bring about change in her community by participating in the process that determines the codes. For right now she lives in her home, and the toughest part about it is "not having that answer" of what issues might come up later on.

Still, Macy lives her life in her tiny house quite comfortably. She feels she hasn't given up anything; quite the opposite, she feels she has gained quite a bit. "There is a lot in that tiny house that I don't need," she said. "It's a whole lot of wanted convenience in the house." She lives a very good life in a well-appointed house that now costs her nothing. All because she worked hard to earn the money and then made her budget work for her.

Photo courtesy of Mark Walters Photography.

Downsizing Luxuries

In her house she has a full kitchen, a standard shower, a queen-size bed, and a full washer and dryer. "[There is] very little that I need in this world, but I've been successful enough and I can afford a lot of excess in that house," she said. It seems funny to hear people talking about excess in a house that most of America would consider a step up from homeless, but it's true.

Before the tiny house, Macy felt as if she were being forced to have more things to show her status as a young professional. Back then she felt "that I had accomplished all these things, so I need to go buy that four-bedroom house to show it." Even at the time she wasn't convinced that she wanted these things; "Honestly I felt societal pressures that since I accomplished this, you need to do this," she said. "The tiny house lifestyle is much more me."

Why Tiny Living Works for Macy

One of the reasons that a tiny house makes sense for Macy is that she is not home that much. With a busy career and active social life she is often out and about until it's time to come home and sleep. With the house built, she is looking forward to spending more time at home in the space she built.

She sometimes works from home now, and she hopes to start up some of her own ideas for a small business. The tiny house will allow her to realize these business ideas because her living expenses are so low, and she can take that time to build her business without as much worry. With a traditional house she wouldn't be able to do that because of the cost and debts.

Now that she is living in her house and saving a lot more money, she plans to travel abroad and see other parts of the world. She will also do some projects that she has always wanted to do and try her hand at some other forms of alternative housing. Right now she is considering straw bale houses and shipping container homes.

Now that Macy does have the time and money, she already feels the stress being lifted. She can work because it's something she loves to do. If she were to lose her job it wouldn't be a big deal; she has all her needs met. Even with the challenges in life that she will face, "There is nothing at this point that I can't handle," she said.

This was very apparent when Macy broke her back. Even though she had medical insurance, the medical bills grew to $13,000 in a single year. Because of having the ability to live in a tiny house, she was able to pay cash for all those bills right then and there; "Otherwise, those debts would have followed me for years," she said.

There are a lot of assumptions made about tiny house people. "It's assumed that if you live in a tiny house you are underprivileged," Macy said. "It is weird how this stigma is, because people can't understand how this could be an intentional choice."

Many assume that you are lower income, less educated, unemployed, and a host of other negative things. In fact, that couldn't be farther from the truth. Tiny-house people on average make more money than the average American; they are twice as likely to hold a master's degree as the rest of the United States, and are 90 percent more likely to have no debt. So it is interesting that a stigma exists. Macy wonders, "Does it take an educated person to live within their means, to be able to provide what they want for their life and at the same time not want that debt?"

Photos courtesy of Mark Walters Photography.

Determining Needs

The one thing that Macy does miss that isn't in her tiny house is a space for projects. Working on her tiny house has brought about a desire to have a workshop. Currently she has a small table that she and friends can eat at, but she likes to do various projects that prove difficult in such a small space. She has thought about getting a work truck that is designed to be a mini shop or portable welding station. Currently her daily car isn't able to tow her house, but with a truck like that, she will be able to do her projects and move her house as need be.

For the rest of her life, the house will provide everything that she will need. When designing her tiny house, she looked to the space that she already lived in. In the apartment she lived in, she noticed that there was a whole room she never really went into. So, of the whole space, she used about 300 square feet and that was enough for her. She then began to experiment. She slowly started taking things out of those 300 square feet and moving them into the room that she never went in. After a month of not having something, she realized she didn't need it. There were some things that she brought back, but by and large her space became less cluttered. This exercise prepared her for tiny living.

There were some things that she knew had to be tweaked. Her desk in her old place was just a little too small now that she was working from home more. Her bedroom was way too big for her needs. She didn't ever spend time in it except when she was sleeping, which meant she was only using the space of the mattress. Her closet was small, so she made her tiny house to have a slightly bigger closet.

In this experiment she was able to determine her needs and also "become more comfortable with those choices." That confidence translated into her design, and her house suits her perfectly. Once she knew her needs, she found her trailer and then purchased her windows so she could design the space to have lots of cross-flow ventilation. She also wanted to have two doors for ventilation and egress reasons.

The trailer drove a lot of the design. When she decided to build a tiny house, she knew before she spent time designing that she needed to know what trailer she would have. Within a week of making the decision, she was the proud owner of her trailer and the designing began. Because of the gooseneck trailer, she had to put the bed in the top of the trailer, which then led her to place her living space. Finally, her kitchen and bathroom needed to be close together so her plumbing could be integrated into one area, which made it easier to work with.

Thoughts on the Tiny House Movement

Macy has seen the tiny house movement grow rapidly since she joined with her tiny house. A lot of it came from the wake-up call that was the recession. "A lot of people lost their houses and I was on the front end of that." Macy used to own a traditional home with a mortgage—because she felt that is what she was supposed to do—but following a divorce, things took a turn for the worse. "In 2007, I started my foreclosure process." Macy lost her home in 2007 and it was a hard lesson to learn. During the five-year foreclosure process, Macy had a hard time thinking about anything else because the process was all-consuming and it impacted her life deeply. Soon after she finalized everything, she felt she could start moving on.

Most people are still dealing with that today because the foreclosure process takes so long. Once they bring it to a close, they can begin to consider options like tiny houses with the wisdom they gained from that process. So many people lost their homes or knew of someone who did, and the experience has left a deep, lasting impression on them. Because of this, Macy feels the movement will only continue to grow as more people exit the foreclosure nightmare.

She said that when she talks with building code and zoning people in her town, "they are very much aware of tiny houses" and they are excited for the possibility of bringing affordable housing to people and spurring new economic growth in their towns. Cities are beginning to see tiny houses as a viable solution to some of the problems their citizens face. Right now the building code people are on board, but existing code holds them back from allowing it. So it is a matter of time before their wish becomes manifested in the town's codes.

Tips From Macy

- Living in a tiny house will likely reduce your debt and allow you the

financial freedom to pursue your passions. It also allows you to more easily weather financial ups and downs.
- Persistence is key. Building a tiny house can sometimes be tedious, but it's important to lay a strong foundation, even if results are slow to show themselves.
- Work with local building codes the best you can. Building codes are expected to change in the future, but it is a slow battle.
- If you are a woman, don't be afraid to build a tiny house. It can be liberating.

DESIGNING A TINY LIFE

When it comes to your tiny home, it is obvious that you must pack a lot of living into a very small space, but how you do it can be the tricky part. You need to be realistic about what your life will be like in a small space and what you need to get out of that space. A tiny house is only as good as its ability to meet your needs.

As you make your way down the path to a tinier life, you must be intentional about it. That is why I am a proponent of first looking at your needs, then working on the design—not the other way around. It is very easy thing to get caught up in this design or that house, but you need to be sure whatever design or house you choose will meet your needs. That said, spending hours "oooing" and "aaahhhing" over tiny house photos is something we all should do. This helps build your repertoire of design solutions, gives you inspiration, and keeps you motivated … and is a lot of fun.

You Have Choices

Part of what makes tiny living so desirable is that it opens us up to the possibilities that life has to offer. In a traditional home you have options, but it limits some of the choices you make. With more free time, less time spent away from loved ones, and more money to utilize as you see fit, you are empowered to do so much more with life. It is at this point that you may ask, "Now what?" It's a common question that retirees ask themselves when they reach sixty-five, but for those of us who came into the movement earlier in our lives, we may be asking ourselves at thirty!

The question is a big one. It takes time to answer, and the answer may change a few times. It's up there with questions like, "What is the purpose of life?" and "What is the meaning of life?" In midlife, many of us are still finding ourselves, dealing with life changes, pursuing a career, getting married, having kids—or none of these things. At retirement age, we may look back at our lives and realize we had a good life, but want to make sure we use the remaining time the right way. These are tough questions. And in the tiny lifestyle, with fewer possessions, you should now have the time to ask them, explore them, and pursue their answers.

The first part of living intentionally is to understand that you have choices. They are choices with big implications, but they are yours to make. Really think here: What choices are you making every day? You choose to get up, go to work, to do this or that. The choices are sometimes small, simple ones, but you are still choosing.

So make these choices with conviction! You are blessed with the ability to choose—and what's more, you may have many more options than other people because of this amazing tiny life you have decided to live. You are empowered to do what you will, to make every day important and mean something.

> *"Every man builds his world in his own image. He has the power to choose, but no power to escape the necessity of choice."*
>
> —AYN RAND

Making Choices

If you are somewhere you'd rather not be, what are you doing about it? It's a terrible thing to be stuck in a bad place, but a true travesty to not work for a better tomorrow. When you live intentionally, you realize you have choices—and that those choices empower you to be where you want to be, do what you want to do, and live the life you always wanted.

When you take a moment to consider your life and where you want to go, be sure to also recognize the context in which you are doing it. This could be your geographic location, your culture, or even your group of friends or coworkers. You need to look not just at yourself, but the system you exist in.

When you take this broad view, you can make substantial changes to your life. Reflect upon everything: tangible things like housing or possessions, and intangible things like relationships, goals, and dreams.

Do you have friends who truly bring positivity into your life, or do you have a group of friends who are always down? Friends are very important in this life, but you need to be careful whom you surround yourself with. It is said that you become most like the five people you spend the most time with. If you look at it from this perspective, ask yourself, are those five people making you into the person you want to be? Although these can be difficult choices, they are still choices.

Knowing yourself is a lifelong quest. There are many of us who are so busy we don't even ask the important questions. Who am I? Who do I want to be? What is my purpose? What are my goals? What ideals and values do I hold?

These questions are big, but you should take the time to think about them. Even the act of thinking about them, without coming to any answers, is important. I might argue that it is the process that is more important than the actual answers.

One exercise that is very useful is to create a personal mission statement. I have even known couples to create these in order to build a basis of understanding for their relationship. In life, you go to work and have pretty clear objectives; you even write your purpose and function in a job description. If you start a group or a business, you have a mission statement or business plan. In so many places within our lives we are setting goals for others, but why not ourselves?

However you try to make your own personal mission statement, think about who you want to be, where you want to go, what you want to do, and how you will get there. It is taking the time to work through these questions that will allow you to understand the essentials of what makes you, you. In this process, understand that you are pondering some of life's biggest questions. If the great minds over millennia had trouble fathoming the implications of life, understand that you are but one person and it's okay that this will be a work in progress. When you are outlining your personal mission statement, remember that it is a living document that will evolve as life carries on.

Once you have done this self-exploration, you will have come to the point where you must make a choice. This choice is to live life for yourself and those you love. It is not about the other guy or girl, the neighbors, your peers at work … it is about you and those you choose to make part of your life. We need to stop comparing ourselves to others because the truth is that there will always be someone doing better than us—it's a fact of life. The more important thing is to only compare yourself to who you were yesterday and realize tomorrow is your opportunity to do better.

When you have fully realized the gravity of making the choice to live life for yourself, you can begin to examine what you want out of this life. It is about making goals for yourself so you can see a better tomorrow and know how to act today to achieve it. In order to make progress, you need to know what direction to head. Even a path has two directions—and without a guide you might walk away from your destination.

Charles Finn

Photos courtesy of Charles Finn.

The Blue Room tiny house by Charles Finn.

Write Your Personal Mission Statement

Write down five of your personal strengths or virtues.
_____
_____

Write down five of your personal weaknesses or challenges.
_____
_____

What are your priorities in life?
_____

Think back to your best times: What made you happy? How did you handle things? What did you learn?
_____

Think back to your worst times: How did you react to a problem or struggle? How did that impact you as a person?
What did you learn?

What do you consider your personal identity to be? What would you like it to be?

What regrets do you have? Is there a way to avoid repeating them?

Who is important in your life? How do you make space for them?

The space far outside of your comfort zone is where the magic happens. Write your final mission statement here.

Setting Goals

Setting goals is an important part of living intentionally: without them you will struggle to find purpose. There are no rules as to what your goals might be, but they are as personal and unique as you are.

When setting goals, you can pull a page from the business world to help you define your goals and see to their completion. What follows is a method I've used to increase the likelihood that goals will be completed. This method reminds you that goals should be *specific, measurable, attainable, realistic,* and *timely* (SMART).

SPECIFIC

When you make a goal, it should be very specific so you get to the heart of the issue you are trying to address. General goals are often moving targets, and it can be hard to see a clear path on how you are going to achieve them. When goals aren't specific, it often means they are rather large, unwieldy, and can become overwhelming. Because a goal is lofty and large doesn't mean you can't strive for it, but it does mean you must break it down into small components. Take, for example, building a tiny house. You can easily get overwhelmed because it is such a huge job. If you instead break it down into ten small goals, the goals become more manageable. For example, tasks that need to be accomplished to build a tiny house include: determine needs, determine a design, purchase plans, learn basic building skills, purchase a trailer, and frame the floor. These smaller tasks allow you to be intentional about achieving them, and also make the ultimate goal more manageable.

Charles Finn

Photos courtesy of Charles Finn.

The interior of this tiny house by Charles Finn in Missoula, Montana, features reclaimed beams and a loft space over a work area.

MEASURABLE

Making sure a goal is measurable means you should set objective measures to measure your work against. An easy part of a goal to make measurable is the financial aspect. If you hope to build a tiny house, at some point you are going to have to create a budget so you know what it will cost you and thus, how much you need to save each month. Other goals that are quantitative and easy to measure might be to visit one foreign country a year, or to only work thirty-five hours a week and spend the time with family, or to read ten books this year.

Whatever your goal, you should make sure you can measure how far you've come and how far you've got to go, and then you'll know when you have arrived.

ATTAINABLE

When you are setting goals, it is important to set yourself up for success. To be unprepared when an offer comes your way is a terrible shame. There are some things in this life that are simply not achievable—and it's important to recognize that—but when it comes down to it, you can do many things today to better your odds for success tomorrow. By being ready, you'll be able to take advantage of circumstances in order to achieve your ultimate goal.

For example, if you really want a particular job that is very hard to get, what is one thing that you can do to increase the likelihood of getting it? It might be that you seek a certification that only 10 percent of the people in the industry have because it's hard to get. Achieving that goal instantly puts you ahead of the other 90 percent of people. After that certification, you might volunteer to take the lead on a project at work that could give you a greater edge or useful experience.

The point is to understand that by achieving smaller goals and being strategic about the goals you set out, you can narrow the pool and increase your odds of success. It also means preparing for the day that the goal is achieved. You want to be ready to seize the opportunity when the day comes that you will be able to accomplish your goal: You want to be able to say, "There wasn't anything else I could have done to be more prepared." "What ifs" in life are toxic, so try not to have them.

REALISTIC

When you are setting goals for yourself, choose goals that you are both willing to pursue and able to pursue. You can set your own expectations on what is realistic for you to achieve, but be sure that your goal will show substantial progress. For larger goals, it is all right to break them down into smaller goals, but they should still be something you must strive for. Remember that in many cases a realistic goal that is lofty can often be more successful than an unrealistic easy goal because there is more motivation to complete it.

TIMELY

Each goal that you set for yourself should be grounded within a time frame. This is an objective measure by which you can evaluate your progress, build motivation, and create a sense of urgency for completing your goal. An open-ended goal is a goal that is often never completed … or, if it is, it takes way longer than it should have. The motivational function of setting time frames cannot be understated. When you have an open-ended goal, you tend to rationalize putting off the work until later.

Long-term time frames can suffer from procrastination, so if you have a goal that is going to take a long time, consider building milestones into your time frames. This will segment a much larger task and span of time to help you gauge your progress more accurately and will let you know when you need to play catch-up.

When you are setting time frames, understand that you don't have to stick to them 100 percent if you run into a major roadblock. If you do experience a major setback, consider what other tasks you can work ahead on to make the best use of the down time, or make it your primary goal to overcome the obstacle. In the end, you answer only to yourself, so you know what is okay to relax on and what needs persistence.

Following these principles will help you design your goals in ways that will set you up for success, in ways that will motivate you and keep it realistic. While these parameters may seem very formal at first, you will begin to understand how to incorporate these things naturally. In time, you won't be sitting there with your SMART checklist, but you will notice when something seems out of tune. If you find that you are having a difficult time keeping to a goal or it seems elusive, that's a clue that you might need to examine your goals and tweak them accordingly.

Another aspect to consider when you are living an intentional life is quality of life. When you make decisions, you probably weigh the pros and cons of that decision and consider what it will cost you, and what you will get out of it. You may not consider how it will impact your quality of life, but this is very important. When you think about doing something, buying something, or saying yes to something, think about how it might impact your quality of life. Will it bring a lot of unneeded stress into your life? Will it get you closer to your goal? Will it take time away from hobbies or time with loved ones?

Saying "No"

The final part to living intentionally that many people don't consider is the simple power of saying "no." It isn't a common word in our culture and it has been almost demonized today. Living intentionally is not just what you choose to do with your life, but also what you choose NOT to do with your life. You must make active decisions on the things you want to pursue, but you also need to realize that sometimes things that you don't want to turn down are actually obstructing your goals.

Saying "no" can be a tricky thing in our culture. We have a lot of pressure to live up to expectations placed upon us by others. At the beginning of this section on living intentionally, we talked about understanding that you exist in a system, in a culture, in a society, in a context—and each of these things have an impact on your life. So when you make decisions about saying "no" to things, consider the broader picture at the same time.

When thinking about what you can say "yes" to and what you need to turn down, think about it in not just the context of time spent, but also the amount of energy it will require. Like time that has a finite amount, twenty-four hours in a day, energy also has a finite amount.

Each day you only have so much mental focus you can bring; some days you are on point and can focus a lot, other days it just isn't in the cards. So when you think about what you are going to take on, understand not only the time commitment it will involve, but also the energy it will tap. There are some things that are really simple for you: They don't require a second thought. There are other things that require a lot of mental energy and focus for you to achieve. So, while evaluating energy, consider not only how much you have to offer, but how much that task will tap.

The interesting thing about energy is that some activities are very restorative or invigorating; it means that as you do them, even if they are very energy intensive, they build momentum. You will see this when you are engrossed in something that is really interesting or that you are passionate about—you look up, and it's hours later. This type of energy rejuvenates you and helps you bounce back. There are a lot of activities that can achieve this, but they often require time. So be wise in how you decide to spend your time: on energy-sapping activities or on energy-creating activities.

For many people, it is obvious what activities are needed to help us bounce back from an activity that requires a lot of energy. Many people are familiar with the need to come home from work, change clothes, and zone out for a little bit before tackling dinner or going out with friends. Things like exercise, meditation, sleep, vacations, and time alone all can be useful to help rebuild your energy reserves.

Different people and different personality types recharge in different ways. Extroverts tend to thrive on personal interaction and their energy builds with it. Too much time alone can make extroverts restless, but it's important for them to be sure to take time to focus on themselves.

Introverts will find solitary time to be an effective way to recharge. While they value time with others, they know their limits and aren't able to draw a lot of energy from a crowd. So they have different relationship dynamics and, as opposed to extroverts, alone time is a grounding thing for them.

Whichever type of person you are, remember to take time to rejuvenate yourself, in whatever form that might take. Learn to prioritize your time and spend it on the things that are most important to you.

Case Study: Lee Pera and Jay Austin of Boneyard Studios

Photo by Paul Burk Photography, courtesy of Brian Levy.

How It All Started

Boneyard Studios is a unique tiny house project where several people have gotten together and decided to build their tiny houses in a community. The houses are each individually owned and serve as a showcase for urban infill. My interview was with two of their members, Lee Pera and Jay Austin.

For Lee, tiny houses were always a very attractive option because she had always been moved around, ever since she was a child. Growing up overseas, she moved every few years. It was a life that suited her well. Later on, as Lee pursued her career, she found herself in Washington, D.C. But at the same time, she found that she "wanted her own home and own foundation, but not wanting to invest in real estate," she said. D.C. is known for its high cost of living, and to buy a home that she wasn't sure she would live in forever didn't make sense.

Because of this, tiny houses made a lot of sense for a younger person who needed the flexibility of a tiny home and at a price that was affordable in a very expensive city. Soon after having the idea, she met Brian and Jay, who were also interested in tiny houses, and they began to look for some land to purchase.

For Jay, it was really important to have a home that afforded him financial freedom, gave a sense of place, and was sustainable. Jay spends a lot of time traveling and because of that he wanted to have a home, but like Lee, wanted the flexibility to take his home with him later if he were to move.

He also knew that he was already shifting to a life that was much more basic. For a long time he had shifted how he lived to what he described as "Thoreau-vian" life. He had begun seeking a simpler life before he discovered tiny houses, so it was a great match for him.

Photos courtesy of Jay Austin and Lee Pera of Boneyard Studios.

How Boneyard Was Founded

Lee came upon tiny houses after attending a straw bale house-building workshop. She quickly realized that having a straw bale house on a foundation in the middle of nowhere wasn't going to work for her. So she started researching similar ideas and finally came upon tiny houses. For a long time Lee tried to find others who wanted to do the same thing. Finally, one day on the bus she made the decision that she was going to build a tiny house in the city even if she had to do it alone.

As fate would have it, that night as Lee laid her plans, a blog post came across her screen about two single mothers who had built tiny houses in D.C. She instantly connected with them and found a lot of inspiration to make her dream a reality. It was soon after that she met the rest of the people who would later form Boneyard.

As mentioned, Jay had already started minimizing his life before he learned of tiny houses. Each month he would go through his possessions and consider them. After a while he only had what made him happy and it meant that his apartment was quite bare. So he knew that the apartment that he was living in, which was considered small for D.C., was actually too big for him. That led him to research some alternatives and eventually to discover tiny houses online.

Jay, Lee, and Brian later connected at a local bike event that they all happened to attend and they soon discovered that they had a common interest in tiny houses. From there, things progressed quickly. Later that year they found a piece of property in D.C. that seemed to suit their needs very well. It shared a property line with an old graveyard, so the name Boneyard Studios came to be. When word got out about their project, many people became very excited. They were contacted by someone who needed a place to park a tiny house for a while and that enabled Boneyard to jumpstart things—using that house as a vehicle to build community around it.

Later that summer they cleared the lot and started building their tiny houses. Elaine became the final member of their group when she contacted them and asked if she could move her tiny house there. Boneyard was then comprised of four houses, a community garden, a shipping container for storage, a fire pit, and a patio.

Photo courtesy of Jay Austin and Lee Pera of Boneyard Studios.

The Build Process

Currently, Jay is the only one living on the property, with the rest soon to follow. Jay told me about his experience building his tiny home. He was surprised how much he enjoyed the creative process. The other thing that surprised him was the emotional aspect of it. "The emotional toll of it all —I did not have any idea how emotionally and temporally taxing it would be," he said.

When he first started, he thought it would take only a few months and he'd be living in his new home. "It's the time it takes, the effort it takes, the level of decision making and decision paralysis," he said. It wasn't something that he had ever anticipated. Lee agreed with Jay that there is often a sense of guilt hanging over them if they weren't spending time building their houses.

At first Lee was worried about the physicality of building a tiny house as a first-time home builder. "We were the most intimidated by the physical aspect of the build, but the emotional aspect has by far been the most challenging," she said.

Even though they loved building their tiny houses, they both learned that these things take time and take a toll on you. It is said that the things in life most worth accomplishing are the hardest—and tiny houses would fall into that category for those at Boneyard.

Another lesson they learned was that in building a house, there sometimes is more than one right answer on how to build things. This surprised Lee; "As a novice builder I always wanted one right answer." But things didn't work that way when it came to building her tiny house. It caused some angst because, as a new builder, she couldn't always see what impact a decision would have down the line.

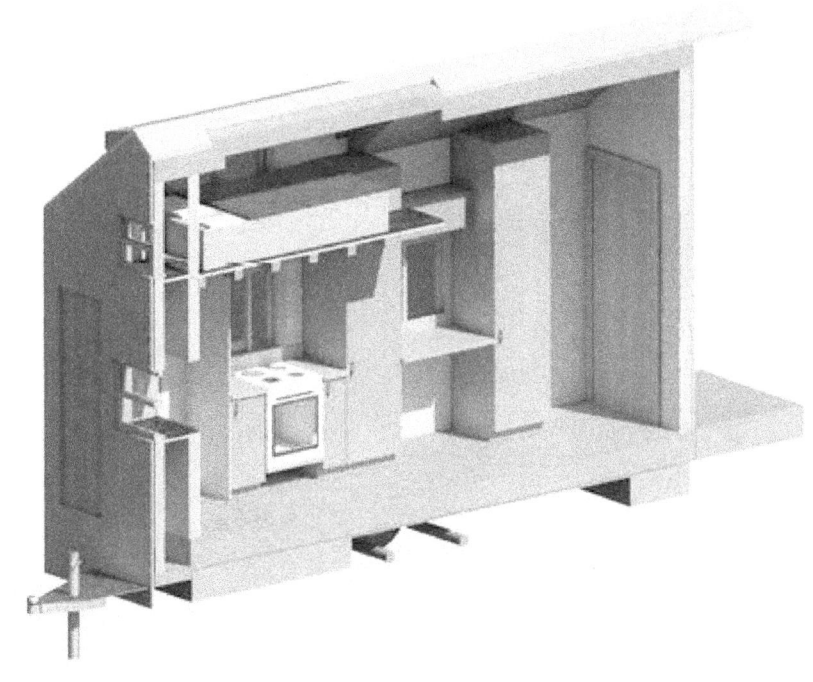

Images courtesy of Jay Austin and Lee Pera of Boneyard Studios.

The Design Process

When it came to the design portion, both Lee and Jay decided to make their own designs instead of purchasing plans. Their houses are unique and designed for their own lives. Lee knew from growing up overseas that she didn't need a whole lot of space; the more space she has, the more clutter she has in terms of possessions as well as in terms of mental clutter that prevents her from focusing on things she wants to focus on.

Jay spent about six months in the design process for his house. He tried various experiments in his apartment to determine if he could get by without something for a month. Through that process he was able to learn what he needed to live comfortably and what things weren't negotiable. Trying out different things in his old space allowed him to home in on what his new home needed to have.

His house is designed to hold all the possessions he has pared down to during his process of getting ready to live tiny. His storage is actually designed to hold more than he owns for a buffer if he decides to buy something new, for a partner, or if a friend were to visit. On the outside of his house he has built an extra storage space that will allow for more overflow, but also keep things that he doesn't use very often, such as camping gear or tools.

For Lee, she looked to other tiny houses for design inspiration and to see how others did things, but also considered what wouldn't work for her. A key element of most tiny houses is the loft, but Lee knew that the traditional loft in a tiny house was going to be too small for her to be comfortable in. She wanted her kitchen to be open so she could cook and talk with friends while entertaining.

Another feature often found in tiny houses is a deck, but she didn't want to give up that much space to a deck, so she designed a removable deck that extended beyond the trailer. For her clothes, she plans to switch out her wardrobe twice a year so she can keep her closet smaller, but still enjoy having a variety of clothes to wear through the various seasons. Shoes are another thing that Lee has made concessions for. She has a lot of them, so she designed special storage boxes to help keep them neatly tucked away.

Lee does plan to have some storage outside of her tiny house for things that she doesn't use often but she'd like to keep. "My original goal was never to have all my stuff in my tiny house," she said. "I always assumed that I'd have a place to store some things or a storage unit. I have a few bikes and a lot of camping gear, but it was never in the plan to have it all in my house, but instead just the bare essentials."

This approach is very similar to many other tiny house dwellers, where they keep the items that they use every day in their tiny house, but often have bulk storage space for a few items that they don't need all the time, clothes that they change out seasonally, or bulky items like bikes or tools.

Lee is working with a few professionals to help her throughout her build: "Tony, a builder of over ten years, Robin, a master electrician of thirty years, and my architect who built a small house for the Solar Decathlon. All have said that tiny houses on wheels challenge them. It is still a building, but there are decisions that come along in the process that you don't realize will affect other decisions later on."

Photos by Paul Burk Photography, courtesy of Brian Levy.

Lifestyle Changes

Jay now lives in his house full time. "I realized that it definitely changes what you can do," he said. Because of this change, Jay has entered into what he calls "part-time retirement" where he works a limited time out of the year and then spends several months traveling. This past spring he took two months to explore the United States on an extended road trip. In the coming year he will be spending three and a half months in Europe, all the while not having to worry about expenses as much. "Because I'm now saving $1,500 a month in rent, that's a trip almost every month that I am saving," he said. What is great is that he is able to take these trips and to save this much while still saving for retirement, paying taxes, and paying for other things that come with being a responsible adult.

Lee is expecting to have a similar situation when she finishes her house very soon. One of the reasons that she started down this road was that she had taken trips and unpaid leave before. Living in a tiny house would allow her to do more of that. She is also looking forward to being able to take a step back from her job and possibly work half time or freelance for less time. Doing so would allow her to pursue her passions that she might not otherwise have been able to pursue.

Right now Lee wonders what she is going to do with all her free time once the house is completed. For the past year she has been working every weekend on the house. After it is finished, that will be a major change. Jay, by comparison, spends his weekends at Boneyard helping others or reading a book.

Photo Paul Burk Photography, courtesy of Brian Levy.

A Tiny House Community

Now that the community of Boneyard has started to develop, it presents an interesting set of circumstances for the members. Since it has been a community focus as well as a meeting place to host gatherings on tiny houses, biking, gardening, and many other things, people forget sometimes it's their home, too. Even living in the community, Lee sometimes has a moment of pause and thinks twice about just knocking on the door to see if it's all right to come over. There are some blurred lines between a public place and a private residence. Many people want to come and tour the tiny houses at all hours of the day, but these are also people's homes. The excitement shows when friends, family members, and others show up to just say "hi" or want to hang out. It leads to a lot of impromptu gatherings where people will congregate around the fire pit, help out in the garden, or just enjoy the green space they have created. So Jay and Lee have had to strike a careful balance between supporting people's excitement for tiny houses with the need for alone time and personal space.

Even beyond life at Boneyard, Jay and Lee both have to contend with being "the tiny house guy" and "the tiny house girl." In social circles many people introduce them as such, which is fine, but there are times where they just don't feel like talking about the tiny house, explaining the reasoning behind it and all that goes with the life. Lee has started saying to her friends who bring it up to the group: "You tell them about it."

So building and living in a community presents some challenges for Lee and Jay, but they feel that the benefits far outweigh the negatives. It's a theme that we have seen with many tiny house people, that while there are some things that come with living in a tiny house that you didn't expect, at the end of the day you aren't giving up a whole lot.

For Lee and Jay, the journey has been an interesting one, a path that has opened up a lot in their lives in ways they hadn't expected. Now they live comfortably in their houses and get to pursue travel and passions in a way that most could only dream of.

Photos by Paul Burk Photography, courtesy of Brian Levy.

Tips From Lee and Jay

- Living in a community brings its own complexities, but it also connects you with others who have similar interests and allows you to share storage, common spaces, and utilities.
- If you have like-minded friends or acquaintances, you may also be

able to share work during the build, making this taxing project a little easier.
- A removable deck is a good idea to increase livable space.

Photos by Paul Burk Photography, courtesy of Brian Levy.

Photos by Paul Burk Photography, courtesy of Brian Levy

DESIGNING A TINY HOUSE

Designing a tiny house is a pretty complex process. There is a huge array of decisions to be made, each with its own nuances. In a small space, every inch matters, as does each detail. Therefore, you must painstakingly plan each aspect of the house. Because every square foot is important, you must make the most of each one.

Case Study: R D Gentzler

Photo courtesy of R D Gentzler of Framework Architecture.

An Alternative Style of Tiny Housing

When people think of tiny houses, they often think of the iconic small house built on a trailer, with cedar siding and a red metal roof. While this is the case for many tiny homes, small spaces come in a wide variety of designs.

In Brooklyn, New York, small spaces aren't the exception but the way of life for most residents. Using the lessons we have learned in the more iconic tiny houses, you can easily apply them to small apartments. This interview is a bit unique in the fact that we interviewed the architect and designer of this space instead of the resident for a different perspective.

When R D Gentzler first saw the space, he realized that he had to be very meticulous with the design because of such limited space. While small spaces were nothing new to him, at 425 square feet, it was one of the smaller spaces that he had designed at the time.

One of the main goals of the design that R D wanted to incorporate was a stand-alone bedroom space. With such a small space he knew that he wasn't going to be able to enclose the bed in a bedroom, but he wanted to somehow delineate the difference between the sleeping space and the living space.

The other important design consideration that he had to make was ensuring that the design reduced redundancy. In a small space, each area should be used regularly by the occupant. Compared to a traditional house where you might have a living room and a formal dining room, in a small space there isn't room for such things. For this reason, the design should reduce redundancy and ideally encourage spaces that are multipurpose.

R D made sure that the space "didn't feel like a dorm room" and wanted to avoid the "feeling of entertaining in your bedroom when guests came for dinner or to visit." Many would achieve this by making a bed convertible like a futon or to hide it away with a Murphy bed. This was one thing that R D wanted to avoid; while the space was small, there was still some room that his client didn't need to spend thirty minutes each day converting the space.

R D said that it was important to consider factors of how his client would interact with the space, and for that reason he had ruled out convertible sleeping options because the size of the space didn't force them to make that imposition on the resident. There are times when the size of the space is simply so small that your hand is forced to use convertible sleeping options, but at 425 square feet, they could get away without such options if they were smart.

They decided to make the main feature of the apartment a single wall installation that would house the storage, an art nook, and the bed space. Most of the storage in the wall was going to be concealed behind doors so the owner could keep things out of sight. Because of the small space it was important for these concealed storage closets to be nonobtrusive to the space. So they used the warm wood of the accent wall to conceal the access doors to those closets.

The bed space was designed to allow only enough space to walk around the bed and was partially enclosed to delineate that this was a stand-alone space. They achieved this by building a partial wall around it, elevating the platform slightly, and using a different wood tone in the floor. All of the visual cues allowed those interacting with the space to understand that it was its own space, a space that was meant for sleeping only.

In contrast, the living space used a dark wood floor that extended throughout the rest of the living space. The darker floors anchored the light woods and white walls, which gave a sense that the space was bigger than it really was. This was important because there were only a few windows for natural light to come into the entire space.

The kitchen was designed to be minimal, with white glossy cabinets and a light backsplash that kept the attention on the main accent wall. Initially R D had wanted to keep the backsplash white to help the kitchen blend in even more, keeping the focus on the wall, but in working with the client, they decided to give it a touch of color using green-backed glass tiles.

The decision was also made to integrate the refrigerator into the wall because of its height. This allowed a cleaner line to be maintained in the kitchen while maximizing the countertop space for preparing food.

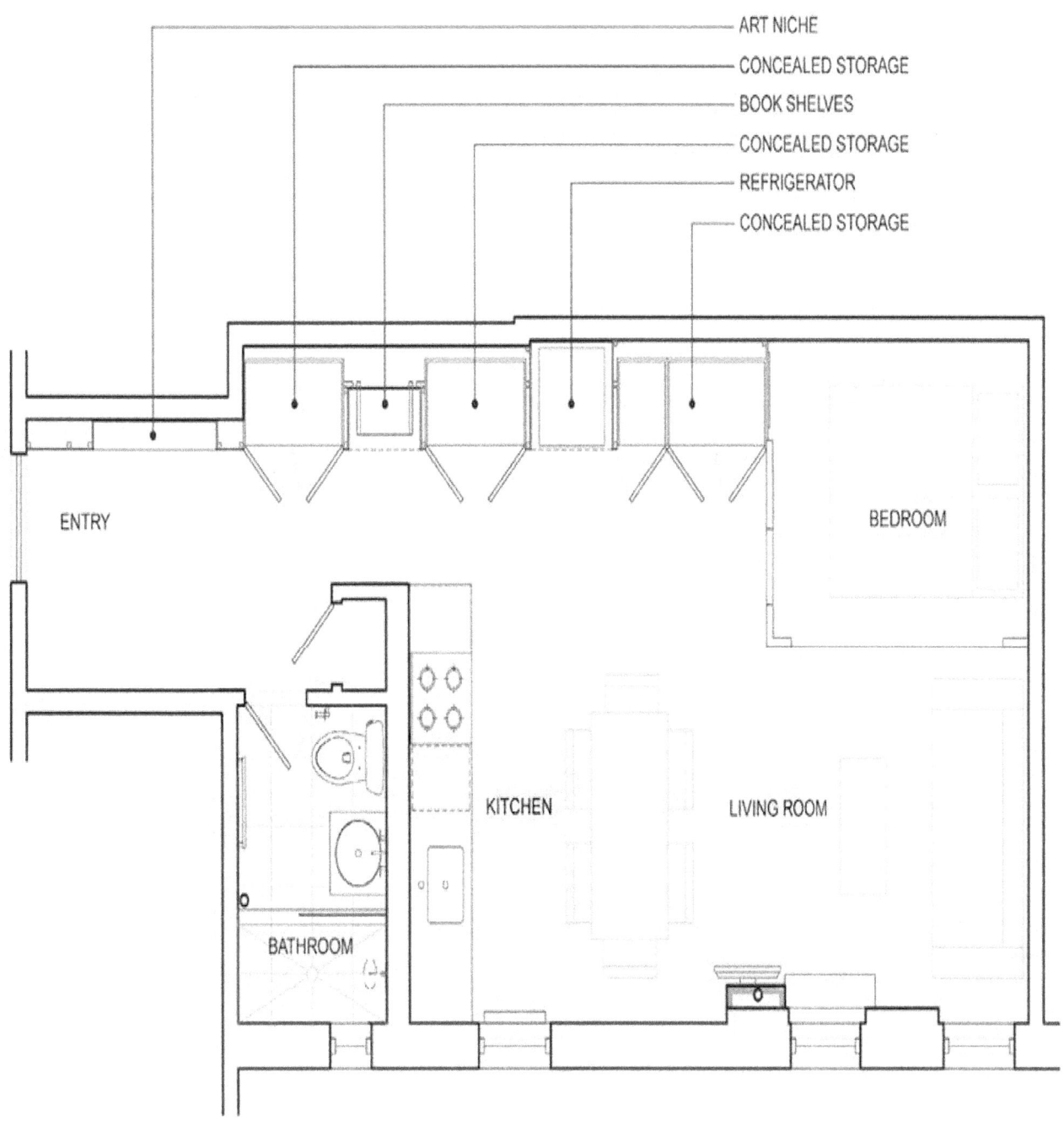

Image courtesy of R D Gentzler of Framework Architecture.

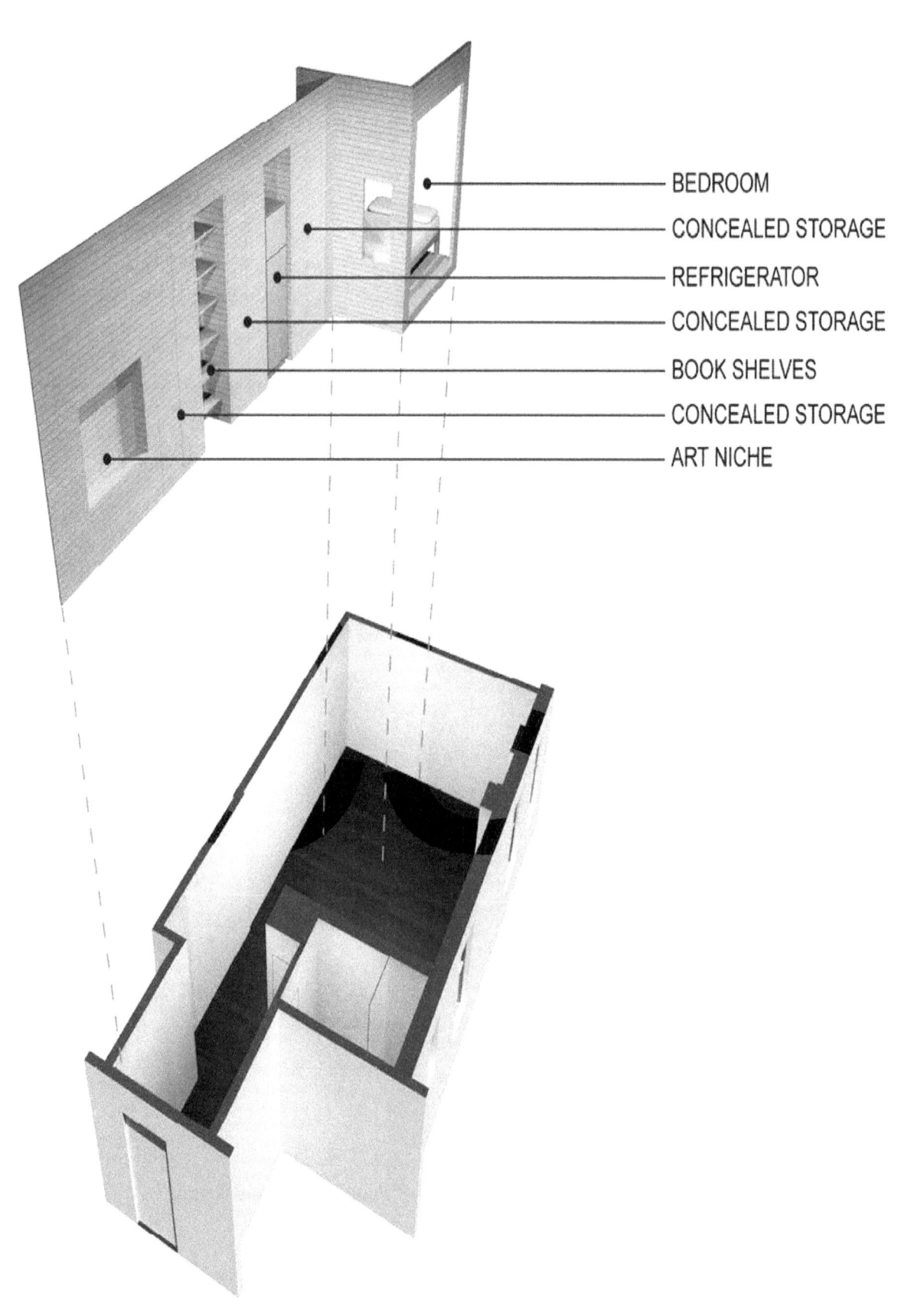

Image courtesy of R D Gentzler of Framework Architecture.

Photos courtesy of R D Gentzler of Framework Architecture.

The Value of Design in a Small Space

Talking to R D about the value of design in a small space was one particular area that I thought this interview might be able to bring a unique perspective because it was from the architect's side of the story.

Most tiny houses are built either from plans or by the owner: We don't often see professional designers enter into the mix.

In a tiny house, even with a small budget, you are able to execute design more effectively because you have the ability to utilize a wider range of materials because your budget goes farther. "If you understand that you have strict budget, small lets you do it more effectively," R D said. Going smaller lets you spend more on materials or design. For some they would rather just keep the cost savings, but overall it gives you much more flexibility to execute the design that you wish.

Most people haven't had the chance to live in a space with good design, but they can feel the difference when they do. Interacting with a well-designed space has a big impact on the occupant. Studies have been done to show that the environment is very important in how we live. R D told me about studies done where students learned in a poorly designed space and then in a well-designed space, and in the well-designed space the learning was much higher.

This also extends to the health of the occupant. Architects are concerned with the impact that certain decisions make on the person living in the space. Architects are well versed in things like low- or no-VOC paint, off-gassing from carpets, and air quality and exchange, while home builders typically are not. These issues come into play particularly in new construction when the materials are brand new and doing the majority of their off-gassing.

Photo courtesy of R D Gentzler of Framework Architecture.

Benefits of Building Small

In smaller spaces you can be more selective of the materials, spend time to research options, and weigh the pros and cons. One great example of this is insulation. Many tiny homes use natural sheep's wool as insulation or spray closed cell foam. Both of these options are more expensive, but at a small scale of a tiny house, the difference might be $100. Compared to a traditional home, using materials like this would be cost prohibitive.

This is something that traditional home buyers have a hard time understanding. Placing a price on design can be a tricky thing, particularly in our current system. Determining the quality of a home in its construction, its materials, and its design are all things that a traditional home builder can choose to share or not, so the person buying it doesn't necessarily get access to this information. Building quality is a very difficult thing for someone to articulate.

Since most people build their own tiny houses, they know exactly what went into the home and how they constructed it. As a builder, you weigh the costs vs. benefits with every aspect, and every decision you make is driven by different motivations than a traditional builder would have. They have to weigh in efficiencies, market demands, price points, and other factors that come into play.

One of the ways you can evaluate a traditional home is through emerging energy performance standards that are coming out now. A home that is built, tiny or not, that can perform to certain energy performance metrics allows for the buyer to evaluate homes to a deeper level without needing advanced knowledge of construction. The truth is that even the most stringent standards placed on a traditional house aren't truly sustainable. Because of its sheer size and consumption of materials and resources, it still misses the mark in terms of where we need to be.

Tiny houses in comparison are often leaps and bounds beyond traditional homes merely because of their diminutive size. The average traditional home produces about four tons of waste, while tiny houses often only produce one to two hundred pounds of waste. Tiny houses that source reclaimed materials can quickly achieve a net negative impact.

Tiny houses and small apartments can also utilize alternative energy much more because of the low costs associated with installing a smaller system. A small space sets you up to a whole slew of cost savings merely because of the scale.

One of the things discussed with R D is how land availability has impacted our housing choices. In places like Europe, Japan, and New York City, land is very expensive, so housing is smaller. However, the vast majority of the United States doesn't face such steep land costs. Lower land costs have allowed us to take money we'd otherwise spend on land and allocate it to building a bigger home.

As a point of comparison, the actual physical space of the small apartment R D designed cost the owner about $500 a square foot, before they even started to build anything. In the rest of the United States, land might cost only $5 to $50 a square foot. So, it's interesting to see how such a great asset of land has led to a skewed view of housing needs in the United States when compared to the rest of the world.

Tips From R D

- Going smaller has many advantages: You may be able to investigate a wider variety of materials, and you'll be able to put greater focus on design.
- Sometimes a space is so small that you'll need to utilize transforming furniture.
- Light is important. Consider how it fills your space.
- Decide what elements are important and need to be highlighted. Also decide what elements might need to blend in.

In traditional homes, sometimes details are left until the very end, and perhaps there isn't as much attention paid to the aesthetic of the home. Today's homes often suffer from being very similar to the neighbor's home because the builder of the neighborhood only allowed people to choose from specific models. There are many neighborhoods in America where the houses are built "on spec" (that is, generically, according to market trends, before a specific homeowner is identified), and in great numbers. What is worse is that the builder is often trying to cut corners—

save money, reach a certain price point, or build the homes quickly—and will make decisions that create a poor design aesthetic.

These houses often have the majority of their windows on the front and back, because if you had them on the sides, you'd realize your neighbor is only a few feet from you on either side. The builder often chooses layouts that maximize square footage and bedrooms because they translate into more profit for them. Design is inherently a difficult thing to put a valuation on and can be expensive, but the impact it has on the final home is so important.

Because the builder is trying to maximize space, you will often find the outsides of the homes look very boring or sometimes even awkward. In the pursuit of more square footage, they are willing to sacrifice visual appeal for a few extra bucks. This often is at the expense of the outside appearance and will impact you subconsciously in ways you aren't even aware of.

Design Cues

A perfect example of this lack of attention to appearances is the garage. In modern homes, a garage is often placed at the forefront of the house, which seems odd if you think about it. When you come to a home there should be a focal point to it: its front door. Having the front door as the focal point is intuitively soothing to the mind. It is a clear distinction of where to enter and it demarks the transitional space of a home from public to private.

Garages used to be detached structures located to the side and in the back of the lot. It meant that you had to park your car, exit the garage, and engage neighbors as you walked to your home. It also meant that the home stood alone in its purpose: It was to house people, not store cars.

When you look at an older house, it often is indeed very pleasing to the eye. With the advent of modern row housing and spec building, builders seeking a way to get more units per acre looked for ways to shrink the lot size to cram more houses in. Garages were added to houses and often placed in the farthest forward position so the builders could add a family room behind the garage. This meant that the builder could shrink the lot width and build more houses.

Another thing about these garages at the front of the house: They often extend far closer to the road, and the front door is set way back. This is so the builder can get two large spaces (garage and family room) in the smaller lot width, but it's also to save a few hundred dollars by having a shorter driveway to pave. An unintended result is that we are confused where to enter the home. It also is a statement of priorities—by placing the garage at the front and the door tucked away, it is akin to saying, "My car matters more than the people interacting with my family in this house."

Along those lines, in tiny house design we often try to employ certain elements of the house to provide visual cues that this is a house and not a shed, not an RV, not a trailer. The successful application of these cues will result in a house that makes people fall in love with it. It is one of the reasons that millions of people who live in large homes see a tiny house and instantly want to know more.

So when you are designing your tiny home, consider how your choices will impact the broader design. It should be a workable living space on the inside, but on the outside should have strong visual cues that this is a house and people are important to it.

"We shape our buildings; thereafter they shape us."
—**WINSTON CHURCHILL**

ROOF SLOPE

The slope of the roof will often help people determine the difference between a house and an RV or shed. When you look at RVs and sheds, they often have very flat roofs. This might be because they are simpler to build, because they are created to travel, or because a flat room is a low-cost area to store extra things. A flat roof or a "shed" style roof are commonly used in these applications, and while generally effective as a roof, they do not give the traditional visual cue that this is a place for someone to live in. Just think about if you were asked to draw a house. What would you draw? A box, with a sloped roof, a little chimney, a window or two, and a door. This is because universally when we think "house," we think sloped roofs.

So when you design your tiny house, while some will want to use a shed roof to give the cue that it is a house, consider the use of a steep pitched roof. The shallower the pitch, the less of a cue it provides, so houses are often designed to have an 8-, 10- or 12-pitch roof to clearly communicate that this structure is indeed a house.

Another consideration when it comes to the roof is your climate. A steeper roof allows for higher snowfall to be accommodated. Because of the steep pitch, precipitation will more readily be shed off the roof.

Flat roofs are notorious for leaking, and while they are a mainstay in commercial and modern architecture, they generally bring a lot of issues when it comes to keeping your home dry.

Green roofs are a popular notion for people wanting to build sustainable homes. There are many advantages to green roofs, particularly the energy-saving impacts it can have on your home. When the summer sun rises high, your plants will flourish, shading the house more; in the winter they will die back some and allow for more exposure. Living roofs inherently bring maintenance and are more difficult to transport because a few minutes going 65 mph on a highway could damage plants significantly.

Many tiny house people also want solar panels on their roof, but while it is convenient, I generally advise a ground stand for two reasons. An often forgotten point of mention is that the effectiveness of solar panels is reduced in higher temperatures. Roofs are often very hot places and when you mount the panels on the roof, you restrict the airflow behind the panel and then get all the radiant heat from the roof.

The second consideration is that solar panels get dirty with dust and dirt from the air and precipitation. Dirty solar panels have been shown to be about 10 percent less effective, so cleaning them is important. When it comes to cleaning them, you are more likely to do so if you can just stand on the ground instead of pulling out a ladder and precariously trying to clean them from high up.

WINDOWS AND THEIR POSITIONS

Windows are critical when building a tiny house because they open up the space beyond the confines of the wall. When you are considering where to place your windows, there are some rules of thumb. In general, you should aim to have at the very least one window per wall and 10 square feet of window glass per every 300 cubic feet of interior space. If you have only one window on a wall, consider scaling it to a large opening.

In the placement of the windows in your tiny house, consider what I call your "common sight lines." These are directions that you are going to be frequently looking at in your tiny house. A good example is the view when you walk into the house from the front door. The farther you can extend that sight line from the front door, the more space the house will seem to have.

Since you will be entering your house frequently, consider where your line of sight goes to when you enter and, if possible, put a window on that wall. This will take your line of sight and extend it beyond the small space to the world outside. It is the purposeful extension of lines of sight that will make your design more effective and the space more livable.

For windows, it is also important to consider their proportions. The ratio of a traditional window is often is 2:3, meaning that it is taller than it is wide. How did this standard come about? Up until now I have spoken about how humans relate to a structure: how we perceive it and what cues it gives us that this is a home where someone lives. Picture a window with a person standing at it. The person will be nicely framed in it, so the window is almost mimicking the form of a person. Therefore, a window gives us a great visual cue that this is a home.

This isn't to say you can't use windows that aren't the 2:3 ratio, but at least consider it for the focal point windows. The other windows might assume the forms of the walls they are set into, or become an accent piece. Whatever windows you choose, keep in mind that it's important for there to be a lot of them. A typical home has anywhere between ten and twenty windows on average, while most tiny houses hover around ten.

SCALE AND PROPORTION

Getting the correct proportions and scale for the elements in a tiny house is really important for an effective design. Without paying attention to sizes, you might find that things don't quite look right. Finding or creating elements with the proper proportions is crucial.

This can be difficult at times because most of the building materials, furniture, and other parts that go into a tiny house are designed to be used in traditional structures. There will be times when you are at the hardware store picking up some material when you realize that its scale or proportions would look really odd on your tiny house because it is intended for a full-sized house.

Recognizing this challenge is the first step, because by the time you get to the finish work of your house, you have a variety of newly acquired skills that will let you execute that material to the proper scale. It may be ripping the board to 75 percent of its initial width, or planning a board to be thinner so it will fit into a small nook. Whatever the case, you will start getting used to modifying raw materials to work them into your design.

Materials

Tiny houses don't require much raw material to create. A commonly cited fact is that the average new construction home generates around four tons of trash in its construction; compare this to a tiny house that often produces only a few hundred pounds or so of waste. So, when building your house, realize that you can choose the grade of your materials. You can use the cheapest materials you can find, or, since the quantity you're using is so much smaller than a traditional house, you may be able to use more high-quality materials for only a minimal price increase. As with any decision, weigh the pros and cons of the actual monetary cost versus the quality you need.

There are a few things that I recommend you sink your money into: your trailer, your roof, and your mechanical systems.

TRAILER

You want a strong foundation upon which to build your house, so I recommend buying a new trailer. I have talked to a lot of people who have tried the used trailer route, and while some of them will be quick to point out how inexpensive the trailer was, it turned out to not be such a great deal. Often they ended up spending almost as much money as if they bought a new trailer.

A common expense for used trailers is new tires and wheels—right there you are looking at around $400–$600. Some people find that an axle that they were told was good and could hold X amount of pounds often ends up needing to be replaced or upgraded. Another thing that I've seen is people putting their tiny houses on used trailers that are clearly not up to the task in terms of capacity. So it is strongly recommended that you purchase a new trailer from a reputable manufacturer.

Eric Bricker

Photo by Joseph Pettyjohn, courtesy of Eric Bricker.

An open concept keeps the space feeling big, while a metal ceiling accent delineates the bedroom.

Photo by Joseph Pettyjohn, courtesy of Eric Bricker.

The custom kitchen island and plate drying rack are made from reclaimed materials.

Photo by Joseph Pettyjohn, courtesy of Eric Bricker.

The metal-clad walls in Eric's tiny house bring texture and reflect light to keep the small space bright.

ROOFING

When it comes to roofing a tiny house, metal roofs tend to be the way to go. While they are much more expensive, you will be happy with the durability, the look, and more importantly, their stability when you are rolling down the freeway—they will not fly off. In many hurricane- or tornado-prone areas, municipalities are starting to require metal roofs because of their ability to withstand the strong winds of a storm. Driving your tiny house on the road causes it to experience winds similar to that of a hurricane.

MECHANICAL SYSTEMS

Finally, the last things that I recommend you purchase new are your mechanical systems; namely electrical, plumbing, and gas. Currently there isn't a good way to reuse old wires, pipes, and gas lines, but even if there were, I'd say always start with new materials anyway. The big things like water heaters, stoves, and heating/air units are things that you can often find used online, but you never really know what you are getting.

The good news is that you'll most likely end up buying these things new anyway because of how niche of a product they are. Water heaters meant for RVs are well suited for tiny houses because they are low power and don't take a lot of space. Many people have tried to use residential hot water tanks or tankless hot water heaters, which can work, but they tend to take up more space than the RV equivalents. This is particularly the case when you start to look at venting requirements of the units, which can require up to a 6 pipe with a foot clearance.

Subtractive Design

A common practice in tiny house design is what we call subtractive design. The design process focuses on how many elements you can remove from a design while still making it effective. It is obvious how this technique lends itself to tiny houses.

When we think of design, we often think about how we can place elements in a space to create the desired outcome, look, and effect. What many of us often forget is that the absence of something is equally important as the presence of other things. It might be the case that the effective use of an element might be highlighted or enhanced without the distraction of other elements.

So when we employ subtractive design, we establish the needs of our space and then look at things that might be removed without impacting the design and function of the space. When it comes to small spaces, anything that is not enhancing the quality of life or the function of the space actually detracts from it. The goal is to achieve an effective design that meets the needs of the occupant but leaves them unfettered by extraneous distractions.

When you are designing a small space, consider some elements in a normal house that are highly under-utilized; you'll find them everywhere. The obvious culprits are things like formal dining rooms and sitting rooms that no one ever goes into. Obviously you won't have the space for these rooms in a tiny house, but what other aspects can you eliminate? Consider transitional spaces like hallways, passages, and doorways. While some of these spaces will be necessary, consider how you might reduce their presence in your tiny house. A passageway might be a great place for you to build your ladder to the loft; it might be a place where you can add wall storage for certain items, or serve as the access point for a closet. If you look at many of the popular tiny house designs, you will notice that almost none of them have any hallways and the only door that exists is to the bathroom.

USE VERTICAL SPACE

After talking with lots of tiny house folks, I have seen this as a trend: Maximize the vertical. Everything above six feet or so is all dead air if you don't use it, so capitalize on that. We seldom realize it, but when we look around a space we seldom look up—we often only look straight ahead or slightly down. You can exploit this quirk of human nature to your storage advantage. The nice part about this space is it affords you storage above your sight line.

By removing the number of items that you can see because you have

raised them above your eye level, you do not get an impression that there is a lot of stuff in the space. For example, you could have a small chest that takes up 2 square feet of floor space. If it is 4 feet tall, you will have around 8 cubic feet of storage. Take that to the ceiling and suddenly you have the same volume, but you haven't given away any more floor space.

When designing these storage areas, consider how it will impact how light enters and flows through the space. Going vertical is an effective tool, but you must use it judiciously. Having some tall portions to your house can make it feel really open, particularly in places where you first walk into. When we walk into a new space our eyes will follow the lines of the room up to the ceiling—this is why a lot of tiny houses have their biggest and most open room be the room that the front door opens into. For storage in these areas, consider storage options that are concealed behind doors or in the storage loft above the door, out of sight.

A PLACE FOR EVERYTHING AND EVERYTHING IN ITS PLACE

As I was interviewing people for this book, one thing stood out to me time after time: People who live in tiny houses have a specific place for everything. Without this principle, your house goes from quaint to cluttered in a matter of minutes.

Make sure every item you own has its own resting place—and be sure that it finds its way back once you're done using it. One woman who lives in a 90-square-foot apartment said to me, "If it doesn't have a place, do you really need it?" and that's a good point. Things that matter and are used are important enough to demand a place in your tiny space. As you're making your plans, make sure to create spaces for these important items.

Many people have told me that when they lived in larger homes, they were total slobs. However, when they started living in a tiny house they suddenly were very neat. It's because in such a small space you don't really have a choice; you have to be neat and put everything back in its place or you don't have room to move. Part of the beauty of a tiny house is that you can put things back so easily because of the small space; you are always really close to everything you need.

DOUBLE-DUTY ITEMS

One popular way for people to reduce items is to substitute several items for a single item that can do many things. You should definitely capitalize on these multifunctional items.

When you consider an item, you should always think about if there is something else that can perform its function already. This may mean you have to create your own items or seek out niche items that can serve this purpose.

Consider a mini ottoman: not only does it serve as a place to kick back and rest your feet, but it can also be additional seating when guests come. Many ottomans also have lids so you can open them and store items inside. So this single piece of furniture serves three functions.

MOST-USED ITEMS DESERVE EASY ACCESS

It is your ability to stack functions in a tiny house that will help make the items in it smaller in quantity and at the same time have more functionality. In the permaculture school of thought— which is a design methodology for ways people can balance human interaction with nature's needs—we see stacking functions as a core design element. Consider the arrangement and placement of each item so it has a maximum effect and reduces labor. This means placing things where they are most often used and easily accessible. Things that you need a lot and use every day should be close at hand.

This seems pretty obvious, but having the most-used items in the front of a drawer, for example, means you are able to access them quicker and without disturbing other things. This really comes into play when you have deep shelves or storage areas.

In general, it is better to not have really deep storage bins or spaces because things just get lost at the back. Think about a deep shelf: You might use a lot of the things within the first few inches of the shelf, but the things in the back often aren't touched for months. However, in some cases, this type of storage makes sense. Perhaps you put off-season clothes at the back of a deep shelf, and then have to dig back there only twice a year.

This type of storage solution also helps you eliminate what is not really necessary. If you notice that there are items in the back that haven't been touched in a while, it's time to evaluate whether you still need them. It's almost a modified version of the box method, where items that aren't touched for a long time most likely need to go.

When you are organizing these shelves, think about what the position of the items is saying about them. After you have lived in your tiny house for a while, the placement of the items will tell a story. It might also be a sign that you want to re-evaluate your goals. If, for instance, you have always wanted to learn to play the guitar, but you one day notice that it has been relegated to the back of the closet, you need to question that goal. If, after examination, you decide that other goals take priority over this one, that's fine. The difference is that you actively considered it, and that is an important part of intentional living.

If, however, you realize that your guitar is on your couch but your textbooks from a partially completed degree are squirreled away, you might want to ask yourself, what does this say? Understand that your items are not only useful, but they can tell a story about your life and priorities, and also serve as a guide for self-examination.

BUILT-INS WITH PURPOSE

Built-ins are nice, but built-ins with a purpose are even better. Think specifically about what items you want to bring into your tiny house. Take stock of those items and let them dictate the form of your storage.

If you are an avid skier, your closet should be able to fit your skis and, living in colder climates, you will need more room for larger jackets than others might. Once you catalog your needs, you can then assign possessions to meet those needs.

Built-in storage and furniture should be well thought out and, if possible, flexible for future needs. As life carries on, you might need to change things. You could gain a new interest, a new job, a new partner—or, since your house is mobile, you might be changing climates.

When trying to figure out seating in a tiny house, traditionally we seek out furniture to meet this need. However, most furniture is not suited for tiny houses because it is too big. So many people look to built-in benches, beds, and tables that can serve as seating in a tiny house. Futons are also very popular options for tiny houses because they can be used as a couch for most of the time, but then open up to a bed if guests spend the night.

GO DIGITAL/PAPERLESS

As if being greener isn't motivation enough, going digital means that you are able to reduce the tangible items you need. Digital files take up no space if you have them stored online, with the added advantage of being able to access them from anywhere. Combined with backing the files up, they become safer than real-world things.

For a long time, bank records and receipts would clutter our desks, but with the advent of online bill payment this is becoming a thing of the past. In the past few years, the IRS has begun to officially accept all scanned copies of receipts and bank statements.

This philosophy extends far beyond receipts and papers, though. For books, we can now get digital versions of them on our Kindle, iPad, or computer. Several years ago I digitized all my movies and sold the DVDs to a used DVD store. You can do the same with music. Long gone are the days where we have shelves of music in the forms of records or CDs. There are dozens of services where you can digitally buy or subscribe to music.

Another thing that people in tiny houses often do is cut the cable, meaning they no longer subscribe to cable television. There are now several really great ways to get almost any TV show, movie, or other media right through your television or computer and save a lot of money. Products like Roku, Apple TV, and game consoles all have ways to connect with numerous on-demand services for free or for fees.

Other things that work well in a digital format are photos. With digital cameras being so prolific in our lives now, photo albums are gone. From time to time we may print out a photo, but in general they all live on our computers.

The possibilities when digitizing your life are really quite impressive, but you must take care that your data is protected. Regular backups are something you should pay special attention to because eventually all hard drives or CDs will fail. The best backup is the one you don't have to remember to do. So seek out options that back up your stuff automatically.

I used to think that having one backup was enough … until one day my computer crashed. It wasn't a big deal because I just went to my backup hard drive. Well, as luck would have it, I discovered that it had died on me, too! I went to my third and final backup and plugged it in, but started to have issues with it, too. After a few hours of work I discovered the problem, fixed it, and was able to restore my data. It is a cautionary story because every single photo I had was in those files, every Christmas, birthday, graduation, party, and vacation almost down the tube.

The mantra of backup is that one is none, two is one, and three is two. Meaning that having your backups in one place is as good as not having one at all. I recommend to clients that they keep their files on their computer, on an extra external hard drive, and then online with a backup service. There are several backup storage solutions that handle all your needs online. While they are paid services, you can often find them for reasonable fees and they are quite reliable. Not only do they provide backups for their clients, but they have several redundant systems for added layers of protection. The added benefit of going with an online solution is that if your house were to burn down, be stolen, or broken into, it is isolated and protected.

LESS IS MORE

So reduce your things, organize your things, store your things. But don't let your things define you. They only exist to enhance your life, and it's important to keep that in perspective. The mentality you need is that of a college student. The dorm rooms are tiny and you are broke. Start from there.

Case Study: Hank Butitta

Photo courtesy of Justin Evidon.

How It All Started

Studying for his master's in architecture, Hank often got frustrated designing large structures on paper only; he wanted to see something he created on paper come to a real-world manifestation. He had his opportunity when he saw that one of his professors had selected a theme of "full-scale prototyping" for the final class project. Hank decided at that point he wanted to try to convert a bus into a living space. So Hank jumped in headfirst, joined the class, and purchased a bus before he even told his teacher what he wanted to do for his final project. When I asked him about his teacher's reaction to his project, Hank said, "He had no idea what I had gotten myself into. When he suggested full scale, he imagined that we'd build a corner detail where two walls come together or maybe a small mobile cart. I showed him a picture of what I wanted to do and he said, 'Go for it!' He clearly thought I was crazy."

So, with Hank behind the wheel, he had to first find a place to park the bus, because he had purchased it on a whim without thinking about where to even park it. He found a place at the school and bargained with a professor to park the bus. From there he started his design.

It was the perfect place for Hank to take his creation from design to conception. The bus was at his school, right outside the school's shop, which gave him direct access to all the resources he needed for the building of his bus.

Photo courtesy of Justin Evidon.

The Build Process

Hank worked on gutting the bus during the day, and then designing the space at night. He was able to get some of the basic work done because it was a necessary step regardless of how the design played out. Things like removing the seats, dealing with the rust on the floor, and insulating the floor space that everything else would be built off of.

When talking with tiny house do-it-yourself builders, there is always one story that today they can laugh at, but in the moment, they almost want to walk away. For Hank, that story happened during the winter in Minneapolis. Hank had used a product to remove rust from the floor of the bus, then had to mop it up to stop the reaction. So he started mopping and when he got to the end of the bus, he looked back to see that the entire floor had frozen over in a single sheet of ice. All the while, the chemicals were still on the floor. After an elaborate plan that involved a makeshift bus skirt and numerous heaters, Hank was able to get the floor thawed and cleaned.

Hank had seen a lot of bus conversion projects so he could tell that, though they met the needs of the occupants, there wasn't much consideration put into the design. Until this point there weren't any designers that he knew of who had really taken on a space like this before. So he came up with some key concepts that guided his design for his bus conversion:

1. Must leave all the windows in place and accessible.
2. Must not build above the bottom of the window to maintain clear head space.
3. Must have simple and warm materiality.

With these guidelines in mind, Hank set off to design his bus. At first his professors where a bit concerned because many of the examples they had seen were not executed well, but gradually they became more confident as Hank's vision came into its own. It took him about a month to complete all the drawings and design work. This included some trial and error in terms of the wall system that he devised.

A key component to his design was that he did not want to have any exposed fasteners or trimmed seams in his roof. He wanted it to be a single contiguous piece. He also had to figure out how he was going to blend that into the lighting unit and then work into the window facing. This was the tricky part for Hank and he came up with a solution after a few tries. He devised a rail system where a single piece of plywood could be bowed into the arch of the ceiling, then seated into a metal channel. Once it was in place, he then tightened some special fasteners that anchored the metal channels and pulled the wood into place—and held it snug.

So once he had developed this technique and how the parts came together on one section of the bus, it was a matter of simply replicating it down the length of the bus. Impressively, after he figured out this portion, the rest of the bus took only a few short weeks to complete. This was mainly due to the fact that Hank had a very clear vision of the design in his head.

One part of the design that Hank knew from the beginning was having a lot of open and clear headspace. He had seen so many bus conversions where the space was very claustrophobic because people built up to the roof. Hank attributes a lot of the success of his design to the fact that he tried not to build above the bottom of any of the windows.

This, however, came at a price. "There was definitely a trade off between comfort and privacy," Hank said. "One of the essential elements of the space was how open it is and all the daylight from the windows. Many bus conversions feel claustrophobic, but we addressed a lot of this with this design, but at the cost of privacy."

Photo courtesy of Justin Evidon.

Living on the Bus

Once the bus was completed, Hank and a few friends decided to take the completed bus on the road to see what it was like to live in it. At times Hank had five other people living in the bus with him on his road trip. At first it was hard because there was no privacy. However, they adapted quickly as a group to compensate for the lack of alone time. They found time each day where they would individually explore the town, find a coffee shop to relax in, or take some time on the roof of the bus.

Even in such small quarters, everyone found a place for himself or herself and a community began to emerge. Someone would be driving, someone cooking; another was cleaning, while another fetched water for the water tank on the bus. This rhythm among the group emerged organically and what normally would be a difficult living condition of six people jammed into a bus became that community. There were, of course, times where people got sick of each other, but the driver's seat was somewhat isolated and people would leave the driver alone because he was driving, so they found time away from the group in that way when they needed it.

The other big shift for Hank was how he had to adapt to the limitations of the bus. It struck Hank how well appointed modern U.S. houses are. "Because you are not really plugged in the way homes are, you really begin to appreciate how hooked up a home is," he said. "You just think it's a house put on a lot. You don't realize that you have water plumbed in and out, and electricity coming in."

It was a big wake up for Hank. People don't realize how much power you are using because it is so cheap. Compare that to the bus, where they had only two 12-volt batteries to run everything. On the bus they had a meter and all throughout the day they watched that meter slowly fall until they had to unplug things. The mini community on that bus became very considerate of each other and weighed personal needs against that of the group when it came to charging laptops, cell phones, and such.

Beyond power they also had to deal with limited water. At the time of Hank's road trip, they had not finished the water system so they were working off of a single six-gallon tank that was connected to a foot pump. The labor of having to physically pump the water made them acutely aware that water came at a cost to them.

Living in this manner helped the group become aware of how lucky most people have it in the United States in terms of being able to flip a switch or turn a faucet, but it also made them realize that there were some things that you could do without or, at the very least, with less.

There were some things that Hank and his group realized they really couldn't compromise on such as refrigeration. For their journey they operated out of coolers with ice. That made them long for a refrigerator, even if only a small one. Out of all the things Hank gave up on his trip, he thought this was the biggest sacrifice because a refrigerator would have made the trip easier, food would have been kept safer, and he could have eaten much better. During their trip, the cooler often left them eating dried goods, often highly processed, or they were eating out a lot more than they should have.

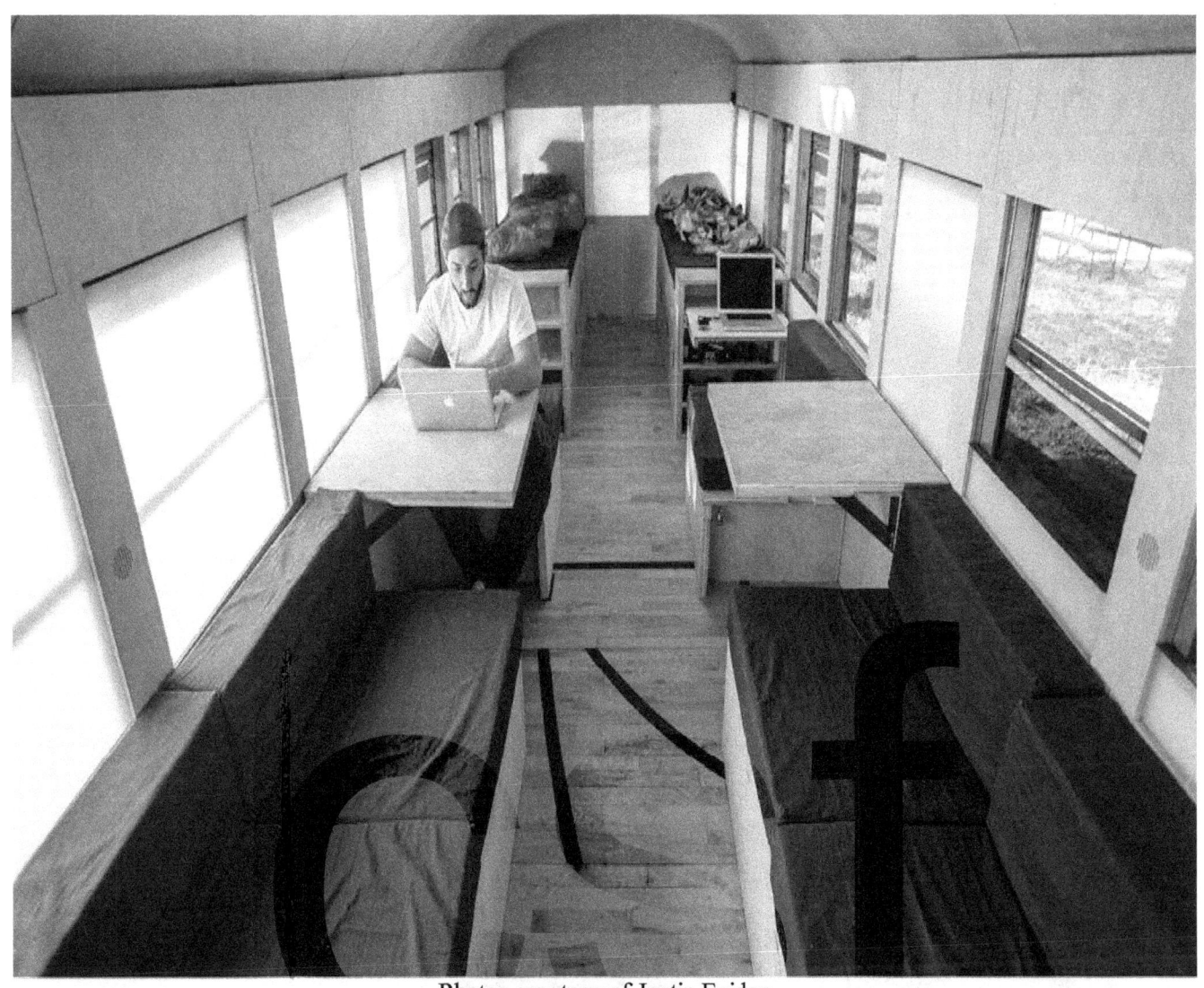
Photos courtesy of Justin Evidon.

Photo courtesy of Justin Evidon.

Lessons Learned

Through this experiment of taking the bus on the road, Hank said he is still trying to find that "sweet spot" in terms of needs and wants when it comes to utilities. They felt that refrigeration was a major priority to add to the bus, as was the case with more water storage. While the bus was a huge undertaking, it showed them how "our needs are so much less than we think they are, but the bus hasn't quite met those yet."

Hank also talks about the importance of accessible housing. While he realizes that a converted bus isn't for everyone, there are other options people can consider. For Hank's project he was able to purchase the bus and all of his materials for under $10,000, which he pointed out was often the amount or less of what people put down for a traditional home. This means that these alternatives are somewhat accessible to the average person because people are able to save up this amount normally when they are considering buying a traditional home.

The advantage to living in a space such as Hank's bus is that he realized he often collects stuff to fill whatever space he lives in. So a big space leads to the accumulation of a lot of possessions, much of which he admits he doesn't need. However, when Hank lives in a smaller space, he is more aware of what he brings into that space and what he buys. He has to be more intentional about the items he keeps because he doesn't have a lot of space to put things. When living on the bus, the bus got "dirty immediately," Hank said. "You can't hide messes because of how small and simple the space is." This meant that while living in the bus they were very aware of how their things interacted with the space.

When it comes to choosing a life in a small space, Hank feels like the decision to live in a tiny house is the real decision, because once you have made it, the space helps dictate your behavior. "I'm not choosing to have less now," he said. "It's more of the fact that at this point I have no option because of the place I decided to live in." That's the key for Hank: It's more about making the intentional decision to live in small space, which then manifests itself as paring down possessions.

When Hank first started his bus, he never realized that it would be of such interest to the tiny house world. He had heard of tiny houses before, but never really spent a lot of time reading up about the movement. As his house gained notoriety, he began to see how his bus fit in with a lot of the ideas of the movement. It was here where Hank learned what the tiny life was all about.

Photo courtesy of Justin Evidon.

Photos courtesy of Justin Evidon.

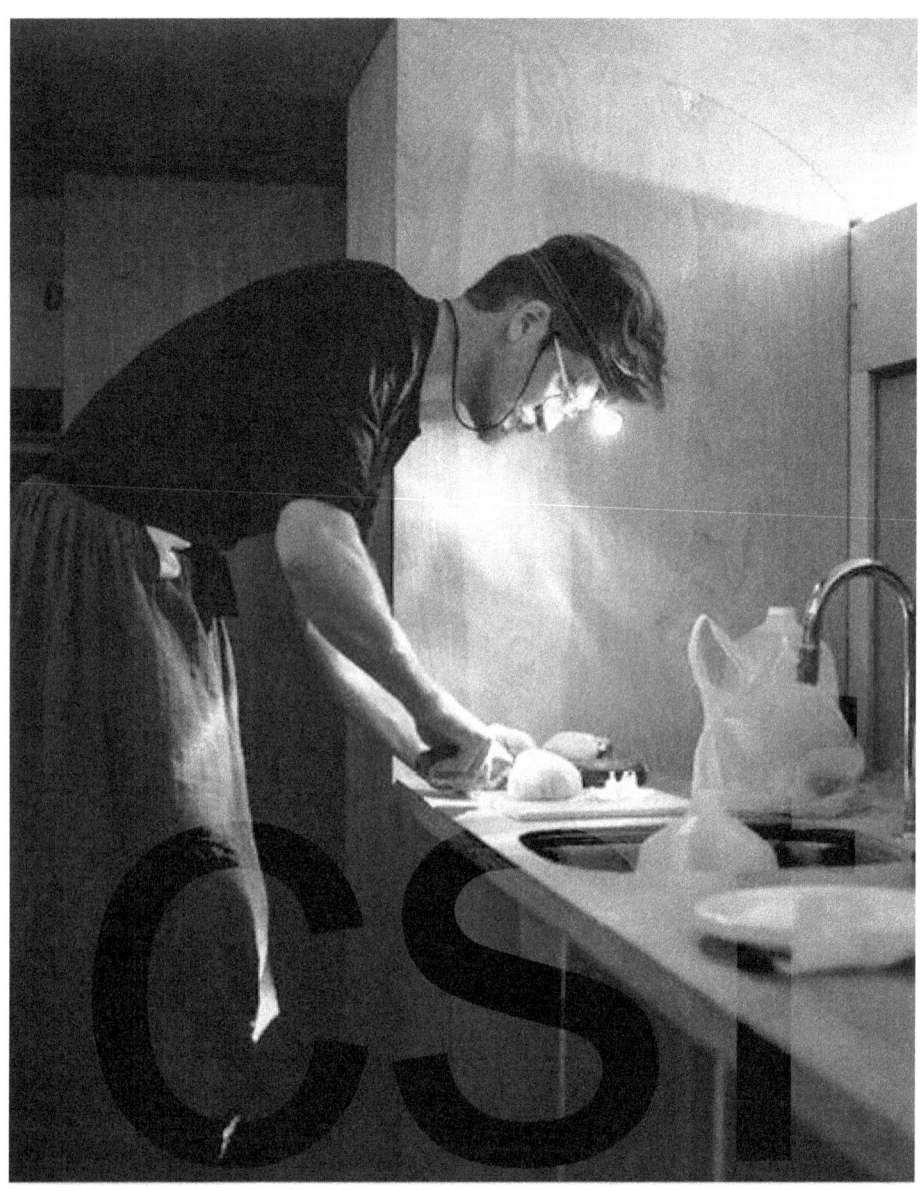

Tips From Hank

- Tiny houses can be buses, house trucks, yurts, and much more.
- Consider storage and your interaction with the space, but don't forget about how those decisions will impact how the space makes you feel. Sometimes giving a little will make the house feel bigger, thus making you feel more comfortable in a small space.
- If other people will share your tiny space, figure out ways everyone can have some alone time in order to keep the peace.

REALIZE YOUR DREAM TO LIVE TINY

People are waking up to the realities of our modern world; having followed the path that many take, they realize there are other options. Tiny houses have shown that it is possible to live a life that is rich with experiences, meaningful, and focuses on the important things that seem to have gotten away from so many of us.

Tiny living is certainly not for everybody, but for those who have taken this path, it seems that we give up so little, yet gain so much. The opportunity of living a fulfilling life draws many people to tiny houses. It's a simplicity in living that seems to "make sense" in a busy world. We give up some space and pare down our possessions to the meaningful and useful for a chance to pursue our passions, dreams, and goals.

It's a life many people can't imagine, but many people also sit in their cubicles daydreaming of a life they cannot attain. The costs of not seeking alternatives such as tiny houses are too great to not act. A dream deferred for many people is the daily life of tiny house dwellers because they acted.

Beginning the Journey

There are many reasons not to act, to avoid change and maintain the status quo, but most of these things are mental barriers. It is true that people will question what you are doing, how you want to live, and the house you do it in, but those close to you will begin to understand. There will be times that you will question yourself: "Am I crazy?" In the end, you and those around you will become more confident in your way of life, maybe even winning over some converts to join you in the adventure.

The quest to simplify is often a very complex journey because it means taking time to understand yourself as a person, your needs, your wants, and how things around you affect your everyday actions. Spending this time in introspection is something many don't have the fortune of doing because they are busy working long days at a job they may not like because they have a mortgage payment every month for thirty years of their lives.

Learning who you are as a person has deep-rooted impacts in many aspects of your life, from your happiness, your contentment, your relationships, and other areas of everyday living. Knowing who you are brings focus to your life, and the effects of that bring about a lot of positive change. People around you notice your confidence in who you are, your ability to bring a lot of mental energy to the projects you take up, and a meaningful connection in the relationships you build.

All of these things will impact your personal life, your professional life, and the opportunities that seem to come your way. When once-in-a-lifetime chances appear, you will have the ability to seize them in a way that might not have been possible in your old life. An opportunity missed is a tragic thing, and at the end of your life regrets and "what ifs" will be the things you'd give anything to change. Don't have regrets. Don't ever have "what ifs."

In the end, you are going to want to be surrounded by the people you love, doing the things you enjoy, and on a life journey that makes you smile when you think about the places you went and things you did. Tiny houses open up the freedom to do all of these things—not just later on, but now.

The ability to do amazing things is something that attracts many people to this life. With a change in your situation when it comes to time, money, and freedom, you now have options. Many people want to travel more, and with tiny houses they are able to take extended trips to distant lands in a way most couldn't imagine doing until they are retired; you are doing it today.

When it comes to earning a living you are able to meet all the needs of the present and the future, while being able to pursue that dream job that might pay a little less. It might allow you to take time off from work to travel more, pursue a hobby, or start your own business. Whatever it is you want to do, you can do, not because you have to but because you love to.

Time to spend as you see fit is also very important. If you could do anything, what would it be? It's a question that is fun to ponder, much like, "If I were to win the lottery, I would …" but the difference is with tiny houses, you have already won. You know what your goal is and you have the time to take active steps to achieving it.

These things that many people can only dream of will become your daily life.

Planning Your Tiny House

Tiny houses come in many shapes and sizes. Their creativity and appealing lifestyle draws so many people to them. Whether it is just an interest in them because of their novelty or because they inspire people to seize a better life, the tiny house movement has inspired millions to think differently about many things in their lives.

There is no single definition of tiny houses, so whatever tiny means to you is the right thing. Tiny houses spur the imagination because they bring creativity to living and housing that you don't find in modern row housing built on spec. Much of today's new construction is devoid of design, is maximized for profits, and buries people in debt.

The ethos surrounding tiny houses is of good design, a dwelling that promotes quality of life and empowers its owner. You will never hear a spec house builder speak of these things, but in the tiny house world, it is all around you. People are willing to look at the impact their home has on those around them whether it is connecting with the community or choosing materials that tread lightly on the earth.

Building your own home is an immense challenge for most people. Having never built anything before, you will push yourself in ways that most of us never have had to before. Working with friends and family to build your home is a unique experience that brings a depth of connection that many will never experience. It's almost akin to a barn raising—not only having a beautiful home that you love, but a home that was built with the hands of those you care for most. This deep connection with your home is powerful. When you are done building your home, you will look back and appreciate it. Most Americans will never have that experience; for them a home is a just place to rest their head at night and keep their stuff. But when you build your own tiny house, you are not just building a house—you are building a home.

It's a home that we seek, one filled with memories and that creates a meaningful sense of place. But it is much more than just that. Tiny houses turn convention on its head and give us financial freedom, freedom of time, and freedom to pursue our passions. That might be the greatest impact of tiny houses—their ability to enable.

Tiny houses are vehicles (literally and figuratively) to a life of your dreams. The ability to choose how you spend your days is something that most people in the world desire. The ironic thing is that when some people build their tiny houses they achieve their bucket list in a few short years! Things that they thought would be difficult to achieve in a lifetime become possible. The question then becomes "What is next?"

Can you imagine that feeling? Having the time and money to do whatever it is you want to do next. What is more is that with the time to do things as you please, not having to worry about so much, you can focus more on the experience. You won't be stressed, always tired, having things drawing your attention away. So not only are you able to do more than you ever thought, but you draw a much deeper value from those experiences.

The Larger Picture

Beyond people actually building and living in them, tiny houses are having a much broader impact. They have brought awareness to the masses about the possibility of housing that doesn't come with crushing debt or have to be in the form of a home that was more than one needed. It sparked a series of questions. Why do I live this way? Is this best for me? What options do I have? What will make me happy? Am I doing this because I'm supposed to or because I want to?

These are liberating questions that en masse make banks, profiteers, and big business uneasy because it threatens their status quo, a standard way of doing things that brings them a lot of money, in many cases at the expense of others. A revolution in housing and living driven by everyday people picking up their hammers to build a better future outside of big business is a big deal.

Empowering people to build their own homes is getting easier. With a host of workshops and resources at your disposal, you can go from hanging a picture frame to framing a wall in a very short time. This is a democratizing aspect of tiny houses, because for a very long time people built their homes, but in the past 150 years, home building has become heavily controlled by government and larger home builders.

With the advent of mass-produced spec housing, the quality of homes has gone down while prices have risen. Decisions are no longer made by the person living in the home, but by the home builder's offerings. The designs that people choose have many elements that are driven by resale-ability and methods to maximize profits. Slowly houses have become less about making a home for you, and instead a house for someone else who would later buy it when you traded up for a bigger house.

With tiny houses, we have returned to sensibility of whom the house is for. It is a return to design, to quality, and to providing not just a roof over someone's head, but a home to build a life within. These ideals had gone missing, but we have found our way back to them with tiny houses. They empower residents instead of seeing them as a revenue stream.

In the end, tiny houses are an extreme. For most people they will be an inspiration in their own lives to lead more sensibly. The rest of the world, and even in this country in the past, people have lived in smaller spaces. Large homes are a modern convention. The ability of tiny houses to inspire, to empower, and to bring about change is the real impact of tiny houses, not the structure themselves. It is the life you can lead after adopting some or all of the ideals that fascinates people when they discover tiny houses.

Realize the Dream Is Possible

It is a life that most people can only dream about. It is a life where you own your destiny, where you seize and value each day. This is your life and you need to own that fact; it is yours, so make sure no one else determines it for you. You choose family, friends, and loved ones over material trappings.

I am reminded of a conversation I had with Dee Williams, one of founders of the tiny house movement, when I first started building my tiny house. She said to me, "At the end of your life, you aren't going to be lying on your deathbed asking for that knickknack you bought at some mall. You are going to want to be surrounded with the people you love, people you have had an amazing life with." It is so true. There are things in this life that are important, and there are things that are not. It's important to remember to distinguish between them.

However you live your life, live it with intention. Each day is precious; we should treat it as such. Our time on this earth is short, so prioritize the things that make each day worth it. Whatever that is for you, own it.

Taking the First Step

When it comes to taking that first step toward living a tiny life, there are many things that can hold you back: not enough money, not enough time, not enough confidence. I have come to realize that most of these obstacles are in our heads. Some tiny house builders, who by all measures had no chance to be successful, have been able to go from nothing to an amazing tiny home.

The process certainly isn't without its trials, but even with the all the self-doubts, the "what ifs," and the lack of experience, people have overcome great odds to build tiny homes—and so can you. Now, more than ever, there are loads of resources for you to learn some of the skills to build your tiny house and a community to support you in your endeavor.

There comes a point for every tiny house dreamer when you realize that the only thing that is holding you back is your fear of taking the plunge. Everyone who has ever built a tiny house has faced the same fear, but they took that leap and never looked back. Once you get into the build phase, you'll wonder why you ever worried about this thing or that. Where there is a will, there is a way, and tiny house people are not just dreamers, but doers.

With some of the guidelines in this book you can start to understand yourself, your life, and your needs. Setting goals is a very strong motivational tool and is critical to intentional living. By owning your life and enjoying the choices it presents, you are empowered to lead the life you were meant to live, not one that society told you to live.

When you live intentionally, it is easy to make a plan. You are able to prioritize things in your life. If you want a tiny house, you must make it a priority. Creating a plan for how to complete your tiny house will ensure success. Even if that plan is to build your house over a few years, at least you made that decision.

Setting goals is the best way to achieve your plans. You can also use various techniques to motivate you and keep you on track. It's something that we don't often think about doing in our own lives, but the results can be life-altering. It is funny how when you begin to set goals and follow a plan, you suddenly realize that there are things that take you away from your dreams. However, once you prioritize everything correctly, it is amazing how the time seems to come to enjoy the things that matter.

Living a tiny life is a simple way of life, but that's the beauty of it. While the pursuit of simplicity is often a complex matter, it has value to it that you don't often find in today's world. It's the kind of life that makes you want to jump out of bed in the morning. It's the kind of life that never makes you have trouble falling asleep at night. There are a lot of things you can buy in life, but peace of mind doesn't have a price tag, and in many cases even the richest man doesn't have it.

Whatever your dream, think about how living in a tiny house can be a vehicle to that life. Making intentional choices in how you live your life is the path to a life worth living—and to the tiny life.

You must pair your goals—your intentional living and your actions—with things that will help you achieve this life. There is the adage: "Insanity is doing the same thing over and over again and expecting different results." If you want a drastically different life, you must do drastically different things than most others are doing. It is important to learn from others, but you must also be able to step back and look at the whole picture. Understand that with small alterations you can make a large change in your life.

So be inspired. Be empowered. Live the life you were meant to live. It is your life to live, so seize it. For many people, tiny houses have given them the gift to do just that.

Eric Bricker

Photo by Joseph Pettyjohn, courtesy of Eric Bricker.

This tiny house was built for a family by Eric Bricker in Austin, Texas. Reclaimed wood was used in the bathroom and bedroom.

The house features a small, open-concept kitchen.

Photo by Joseph Pettyjohn, courtesy of Eric Bricker.

The living room was made with reclaimed lumber.

Large windows extend the small space to the outdoors.

Case Study: Andrea Tremols and Cedric Baele

Photos courtesy of Andrea Tremols.

How It All Started

Coming out of college there was one thing that Andrea and Cedric knew they wanted to do. Having accumulated a lot of student loans during school, they started looking for a solution to help them become debt-free. At the time taking on more debt in the form of a mortgage seemed crazy, but that's exactly what most of their peers were doing: buying big houses.

The other thing that they knew they wanted was flexibility. Being young professionals they could anticipate in the coming years that they would need to move as they advanced their careers. What they didn't realize was how quickly they would have to move. (More on that later.)

Cedric and Andrea first found out about tiny houses in a bookstore while on vacation. They came across a book that had lots of pictures of tiny houses and they realized instantly it was for them. Soon after they picked up a tiny house-building guide called *Go House Go* by Dee Williams. That guide allowed them to figure out the technical parts of the tiny house. Armed with that knowledge, they felt like tiny houses were a very achievable dream.

One day they found themselves taping out a rough floor plan of the tiny house they wanted to build on the floor of their apartment. "We had just gotten back from traveling and we had almost nothing, just a backpack each," Andrea said. So they stood there in the nearly empty apartment and considered the life they could live in their tiny house that they had laid out on the floor.

Soon they started building their house. They purchased a used trailer and found a place to park it—at a local nonprofit that reclaimed lumber from old homes. The space was perfect. There was a large warehouse to build in, and if they volunteered so many hours a month at the nonprofit, they could use as much of the reclaimed lumber they wanted for free.

Approaching the Build

Cedric did have a leg up when it came to building the tiny house. Formerly he was a professional boat builder, so he was used to using tools, building large projects, and designing small spaces. When they first started building the tiny house, Andrea worked a day job while Cedric worked full time on the house.

So, with a few months of hard work, help from friends, and some patience, they quickly had a house to live in. During the build they realized how much they really came to love and value their community and friends. People offered to come help them with their house, and they ended up building a little community around their tiny house that had they never expected.

Andrea and Cedric didn't buy plans for their tiny house because of their use of reclaimed materials, most of which were odd sizes and lengths so it would be hard to match up what they had on hand with what the plans called for. So they laid out a basic floor plan and went from there.

Their house ended up being about 90 percent reclaimed. "It would be hard to do much more than that," Andrea said; "100 percent is really impossible." Even with an entire warehouse of materials on hand, it was difficult to get it all as reclaimed because there were key structural pieces that they wanted to be sure could handle the stress of the road.

Working with reclaimed materials took a lot of time, as well. Each board had to be inspected, selected, de-nailed, and then planed just to be able to use it. When you are building an entire house, even a tiny house, this takes a huge amount of time to amass the amount of wood needed for the job. Adding to the complexity was that each piece was a different size, meaning that there was never any consistency to the boards when they got them. They had to plane the boards into a uniform size.

Andrea and Cedric like to say that their house "is made of a lot of different houses, a lot of different lives." It is an interesting notion that the parts of other people's homes, where they built their lives, where they raised families and grew old together, was now their house. The energy from those previous lives was built into their tiny house where they were going to build their own life.

One thing they wished they could have changed was their decision to build within the wheel wells. This meant they could frame their walls quite easily, but it came at the expense of their house being a bit narrow on the inside. Had they known this, they would have built it so the walls partially went over the wheel wells just enough to give them a few more inches.

Determining Needs

Since they had just gotten back from backpacking in Europe, they didn't have a lot of material possessions. At the time they lived out of their backpacks and felt that they had everything they needed. "It made us realize that we don't really need a whole lot to be happy," Andrea said. It was clear to them that experiences and relationships were much more important than the material trappings of the modern world.

When they got serious about building, they sat down and made a list of all the things they couldn't get outside of the house. They also considered things that they needed to do privately. From this exercise they had a short list of what their house had to provide them and based their design off of that.

For them it came down to a place to sleep, cook, bathe, and spend time reading, and they knew that their house needed to do all of these things in a way that was aesthetically pleasing. It was also important for them to build a tiny house that people instantly understood was a house, not an RV. They wanted a cabin feel for their home and wanted the structure to communicate that it was indeed a home.

This worked out well for them because since it clearly looked like a home, their neighbors were much more receptive to having their tiny house in the neighborhood because it looked like a house. Andrea told me how people in the neighborhood came to know them because they were curious about the tiny house. So the house served as a way to connect them to the community. They were welcomed and never had any issues with the city because their neighbors liked that they were people who cared about their home, even if it was tiny.

Andrea told me, "Because you live in a tiny house, you don't have the space for all the things you might want, just what you need." They made up for that by living in communities that they could interact with and find those wants within. In Charleston, South Carolina, they could walk to the grocery store, bars, restaurants, and their favorite places to hang out. It was the engagement of the community that made living in their tiny house possible.

There are some things that Cedric and Andrea aren't able to do at this point in their tiny house. Both of them are very creative people, so the size of the house limits larger projects if the weather outside isn't nice. Andrea also said she had to cut back on canning vegetables from her garden because it simply took too much space. While canning she needed room to spread out to allow the jars to cool and a place to prep all the food that she put into the jars.

They love to cook so they wanted a very functional kitchen. They made sure to include a full stove and oven in the space. With the space dedicated to cooking, there isn't much room for more than one person so it means that cooking is "a one-person affair." They have a few key appliances that are multipurpose, but don't take up a lot of room.

They realized that they really don't need much more. With just two pots and a pan they were able to cook for and entertain six people and two dogs for dinner one night in their tiny house. When they can they have dinner parties outdoors for larger groups because Andrea likes to entertain and have visitors.

Photos courtesy of Andrea Tremols.

On the Move

Living in Charleston, they had settled into a comfy life in their tiny house when Cedric was promoted to be a manager at his company. This meant that they had to suddenly move to Vermont almost one thousand miles north. When it comes to moving a tiny house, things get a lot easier when all you have to do is hitch up the house and go.

They decided to use a transporting service to move their house because they didn't have a good tow vehicle and they could make sure it was insured against any possible damage during the trip.

The experience was very surreal for them. Having only just left Charleston, it felt like they were on vacation, but their home happened to be there. It was a "very bizarre experience because we were a thousand miles away, but it was our house in an incredibly different environment," Andrea said. Adding to the shock was that they left Charleston during the tail end of summer, but in Vermont, the first snow had fallen already. Cedric told me how "for a long time it was hard to adjust to walking out your front door and it being a completely different environment. We weren't in Charleston anymore."

There have been some challenges to living in Vermont. Outdoor living has been limited quite a bit with the snow. They also have to contend with more clothing by nature of having winter jackets and boots. So they like to tell people who want to live in tiny houses to consider the climate and your ability to spend time outdoors.

Life Changes When Living Tiny

Their time since moving into the tiny house has changed quite a bit. Not having to worry about bills as much because their cost of living is so much lower has allowed them to pursue rewarding careers. "I don't feel so dependent on one job," Cedric said. "Renting a house for gobs of money isn't something that I have to worry about."

Andrea and Cedric don't own land yet, but they have been able to find land to rent. Currently they are living on an organic farm where they lend a hand on the farm for a few hours in exchange for rent. It's during these times where they have a place to live in their tiny house that they feel the most connected with those around them.

When they moved they had to consider where they were going to get water and how they were going to connect to power and fill other basic needs. This is a particular challenge for tiny house dwellers who don't own their own land, because the situation can be somewhat fluid. Once you find a place to park and live in the tiny house, you will be fine. But during that process it can be stressful. These days, life is less stressful for Andrea and Cedric.

All in all, Andrea and Cedric feel that the life they lead now is much better. It comes with less worry and brings focus to the things that are important to them. Living in a tiny house has allowed them to pursue rewarding careers, give focus to relationships, and spend more time traveling abroad.

Tips From Andrea and Cedric

- If your house will be mobile and you might travel to different climates, consider a contingency plan for storing more winter clothes.

- Figure out how you can participate in your community and give back instead of just staying in your house.
- Having land brings security, but renting land with a tiny house brings flexibility. Decide what is right for you.

www.ingramcontent.com/pod-product-compliance
Lightning Source LLC
Chambersburg PA
CBHW081047180326
41452CB00010B/331